NATIONS *IN TRANSITION*

AFGHANISTAN

by Hamed Madani

**GREENHAVEN
PRESS®**

San Diego • Detroit • New York • San Francisco • Cleveland
New Haven, Conn. • Waterville, Maine • London • Munich

Acknowledgments

To the Afghans who lost their precious lives so that other Afghans may live in a free and Islamic Afghanistan. Many thanks to my wife, Afghani, and our children Lina, Mitra, Michelle,
and Arya for enduring the time I spent away from them to work on this project. I also wish to
thank Lauri Friedman, reader and editor, for her tireless efforts to improve this book.

LIBRARY OF CONGRESS CATALOGING-IN-PUBLICATION DATA

Afghanistan / by Hamed Madani.
    p. cm. — (Nations in transition)
    Includes bibliographical references and index.
    ISBN 0-7377-1670-3 (lib. bdg. : alk. paper)
    1. Afghanistan—History. 2. Ethnology—Afghanistan. 3. Women—Afghanistan—Social
conditions. I. Madani, Hamed. II. Nations in transition (Greenhaven Press)
    DS361.A33 2004
    958.1—dc21

                                                                    2003054323

Contents

Foreword

In 1986 Soviet general secretary Mikhail Gorbachev initiated his plan to reform the economic, political, and social structure of the Soviet Union. Nearly three-quarters of a century of Communist ideology was dismantled in the next five years. As the totalitarian regime relaxed its rule and opened itself up to the West, the Soviet peoples clamored for more freedoms. Hard-line Communists resisted Gorbachev's lead, but glasnost, or "openness," could not be stopped with the will of the common people behind it.

In 1991 the changing USSR held its first multicandidate elections. The reform-minded Boris Yeltsin, a supporter of Gorbachev, became the first popularly elected president of the Russian Republic in Soviet history. Under Yeltsin's leadership, the old Communist policies soon all but disintegrated, as did the Soviet Union itself. The Union of Soviet Socialist Republics broke apart into fifteen independent entities. The former republics reformed into a more democratic union now referred to as the Commonwealth of Independent States. Russia remained the nominal figurehead of the commonwealth, but it no longer dictated the future of the other independent states.

By the new millennium, Russia and the other commonwealth states still faced crises. The new states were all in transition from decades of totalitarian rule to the postglasnost era of unprecedented and untested democratic reforms. Revamping the Soviet economy may have opened up new opportunities in private ownership of property and business, but it did not bring overnight prosperity to the former republics. Common necessities such as food still remain in short supply in many regions. And while new governments seek to stabilize their authority, crime rates have escalated throughout the former Soviet Union. Still, the people are confident that their newfound freedoms—freedom of speech and assembly, freedom of religion, and even the right of workers to strike—will ultimately better their lives. The process of change will take time and the people are willing to see their respective states through the challenges of this transitional period in Soviet history.

The collapse and rebuilding of the former Soviet Union provides perhaps the best example of a contemporary "nation in transition," the focus of this Greenhaven Press series. However, other nations that fall under the series rubric have faced a host of unique and varied cultural shifts. India, for instance, is a stable, guiding force in Asia, yet it remains a nation in transition more than fifty years after winning independence from Great Britain. The entire infrastructure of the Indian subcontinent still bears the marking of its colonial past: In a land of eighteen official spoken languages, for example, English remains the voice of politics and education. India is still coming to grips with its colonial legacy while forging its place as a strong player in Asian and world affairs.

North Korea's place in Greenhaven's Nations in Transition series is based on major recent political developments. After decades of antagonism between its Communist government and the democratic leadership of South Korea, tensions seemed to ease in the late 1990s. Even under the shadow of the North's developing nuclear capabilities, the presidents of both North and South Korea met in 2000 to propose plans for possible reunification of the two estranged nations. And though it is one of the three remaining bastions of communism in the world, North Korea is choosing not to remain an isolated relic of the Cold War. While it has not earned the trust of the United States and many of its Western allies, North Korea has begun to reach out to its Asian neighbors to encourage trade and cultural exchanges.

These three countries exemplify the types of changes and challenges that qualify them as subjects of study in the Greenhaven Nations in Transition series. The series examines specific nations to disclose the major social, political, economic, and cultural shifts that have caused massive change and in many cases, brought about regional and/or worldwide shifts in power. Detailed maps, inserts, and pictures help flesh out the people, places, and events that define the country's transitional period. Furthermore, a comprehensive bibliography points readers to other sources that will deepen their understanding of the nation's complex past and contemporary struggles. With these tools, students and casual readers trace both past history and future challenges of these important nations.

Introduction
A Country in Constant Transition

For the majority of its existence, Afghanistan has been at a crossroad of civilizations and empires and a cockpit for contests between foreign rivals. Despite this, Afghan people have always violently resisted outside pressure and interference and strongly suspected centralized government.

For many centuries, Afghanistan was an important trade center situated along the Silk Road, which stretched from China to the Middle East. Past civilizations, including Greek and Persian, fought long and bitter wars to dominate and control Afghanistan, and it was because of the colonial rivalry between British India and czarist Russia in the nineteenth century that the Afghan state was created. That rivalry, known as the Great Game, was about retarding each other's advances from their respective spheres of influence in the region. Eventually, they used Afghanistan as a buffer state between them.

Suspicion of Outsiders

The imperialistic ambitions of foreign powers in Afghanistan made Afghans wary of outsiders, which led to xenophobia (dislike of foreigners) and a great desire for isolation from the rest of the world. After years of isolation, Afghanistan went through another transition when the country was drawn into another competition called the Cold War. A new generation of outward-looking Afghan politicians abandoned xenophobia and tried to take advantage of the superpower competition in order to introduce modernization and economic development to their society.

Afghanistan, however, became heavily dependent on foreign powers, especially the Soviet Union, for military and economic aid. In particular, the presence of Soviet forces to bolster the pro-Moscow Afghan regime dismayed many Afghans and, once again, renewed their sense of distrust of outsiders. As a result, many Afghans resorted to violence to expel the occupiers from their land.

Suspicious of Each Other

When Afghans are not preoccupied with challenging foreign intervention, they resort to fighting each other for power. This is because the Afghan society is fragmented with disparate and often hostile ethnic and religious groups. The situation is further exacerbated by the country's borders that divide these groups among several nations. Lack of unity among Afghans encourages the foreign powers in the region to provide support for their own ethnic and religious groups, by which meddling in the domestic affairs of the country.

Moreover, the cleavage of Afghan society into multiple ethnic and religious factions provides a sense of solidarity, security, and political power to the members of each group. For most Afghans, identity and loyalty to one's ethnicity and religion supersedes nationalism, thus preventing the emergence of national consciousness and consensus. The lack of national loyalty among Afghans has resulted in a weak central government.

Afghanistan's Future

In 1996, after several years of civil unrest, an extremist religious group called the Taliban took control of the weak central government in the capital city of Kabul to install their own form of

Taliban militiamen sit on a tank near Kabul. In 1996 the Taliban overthrew the government and established an oppressive regime based on an extreme interpretation of the Koran.

government. They were a well-organized, highly motivated group who believed themselves to be soldiers of God, destined to introduce a puritan Islamic state in Afghanistan, based on their own interpretation of the Koran. The Taliban welcomed foreigners Osama bin Laden and al-Qaeda, whom they allowed to use Afghan territory as a depot for international terrorism. After September 11, 2001, Afghanistan became the focus of the American war on terrorism when the Taliban refused to surrender Osama bin Laden to the United States.

With the fall of the Taliban, Afghanistan has moved into a new chapter in its history. Afghans still feel wary and continue to grapple with the presence of foreign troops. After more than two decades of suffering and bloodshed, many Afghans hope their nation will enter a new period of peace and prosperity free from outside intervention. Afghans have been yearning for the return of peace and prosperity; however, it remains to be seen to what extent their leaders will support the new government and the American-led coalition. It is also unclear if it is even possible to create a strong government of national unity based on democracy and equal participation of all ethnic and religious groups. Until these monumental challenges are overcome, Afghanistan will remain a nation in transition.

The Great Game: Colonial Struggle for Afghanistan 1

For centuries Afghanistan was a crossroad of cultures ruled by different governments. The Mogul Empire of India ruled the eastern and southern parts of Afghanistan while the Safawid Empire of Persia dominated the western region.

In 1774 Ahmed Khan, an Afghan commander in the Safawid army, was crowned king by a tribal *Loya Jirga* (grand council) after his Persian officers assassinated the reigning king. He thereafter became Ahmed Shah (king). Most Afghan historians have called Ahmed Shah the founder of the Afghan nation. Afghans refer to him as Ahmed Shah Baba, meaning "the father of the nation."

Afghan rulers have since attempted to build a strong state in order to initiate economic development and modernization of Afghanistan. However, several factors made the emergence of a strong state in Afghanistan difficult. One major factor of disunity was rivalry between British India and czarist Russia throughout the nineteenth and twentieth centuries. This competition was dubbed the Great Game.

Origin of the Term

Arthur Conally, a nineteenth-century British scout and explorer in Afghanistan, first described the Anglo-Russian rivalry over the country as the "great game" in a letter to a friend. He stated that he wished to play a part in "a great game" to frustrate the Russian schemes to conquer the region. This phrase was later popularized in Rudyard Kipling's novel *Kim.* The novel is about Kimball O'Hara, the orphaned son of an Irish soldier, who thwarts a Russian plot in British India.

The Great Game was the competition between British India and czarist Russia for control of Afghanistan. The Russian czar, who was steadily extending his empire southeastward into Central Asia, saw Afghanistan as a prime invasion route to the wealthy

The bazaar in Kandahar circa 1800. During the nineteenth and twentieth centuries, British India and Russia competed for control of Afghanistan.

British Indian colony. The British, who continued to advance their Indian gains northwestward from Delhi, believed that whoever controlled Afghanistan could potentially dictate India's future. In order to pursue their expansionist programs, Britain (operating from India) and Russia subdued and manipulated Central Asian countries in the area, which became pawns in their Great Game.

British and Russian Interests in the Region

The British interest in the region started in the early seventeenth century with the establishment of the East India Company, a British trading company in India. The company ruled India until 1858 when the administration of the country became the responsibility of the British king. In order to protect India and maintain the stability necessary for trade, Britain had to expand its influence in the surrounding areas.

At the same time, Russia considered Central Asia within its own sphere of expansion. They feared a permanent British occupation of the region as the British moved northwestward and got closer to Afghanistan. Therefore, to effectively counter the British moves in this area, the Russians tried to make their presence felt in Afghanistan by getting the Afghan government to receive a Russian envoy in Kabul.

As India was a great prize to the British, they feared Russia's expansion into Afghanistan indicated their intent to dominate India, and eventually the world. Consequently the British government began closely monitoring Russia's movement in Afghanistan. Subsequent British governments adopted several strategies against Russian influence in Afghanistan including adoption of the so-called forward policy, stationary policy, and creation of a buffer state.

Forward Policy

The objectives of the forward policy were to prevent Russian advances in Central Asia. The British thought they could best accomplish this by advancing westward toward Afghanistan to provide themselves with a natural boundary, the Hindu Kush (a range

> # Early Afghan History
>
> Before the people of Afghanistan were pawns in the Great Game, they endured a long line of conquerors and migrants who swept through the Afghan territories replacing existing civilizations and religions with new ones. Over the millennia, regional neighbors such as the Achaemenids, the Greeks, the Mauryas, the Sassanids, the Moguls, and the Safawids competed for supremacy in the region of Afghanistan. Each empire that conquered the region was soon replaced by another empire. Anthropologist Louis Dupree in his book titled *Afghanistan* notes that "for millennia, the land now called Afghanistan sat in the center of the action, the meeting of four ecological and cultural areas: the Middle East, Central Asia, the Indian Subcontinent, and even the Far East."

of mountains lying from northeast to southwest of present-day Afghanistan). They also sought to bring Afghanistan under tighter British control and away from Russian influence. Historian Vartan Gregorian states, "[The British considered] Afghanistan as a state far too weak and barbarous to remain isolated and wholly uninfluenced between two great military empires [British India and czarist Russia]. We [the British] cannot allow it to fall under the influence of any power whose interests are antagonistic to our own."[1]

The forward policy was first enacted in 1839 when Britain decided to invade Afghanistan after the Russian-aided Persian armies attacked Herat (a city in western Afghanistan) and placed it under siege. The British considered Herat the gateway to India and so viewed the Persian attack as a direct threat to India's security.

Adding to the situation, Dost Muhammad Khan, the reigning king of Afghanistan, played the tensions between the two empires against each other when he received a Russian envoy at his court in Kabul. He knew receiving the Russian would alarm the British about a possible closer relationship between Afghanistan and Russia, and used the opportunity to get Britain's attention and financial support. The king's tactics backfired, however, when Britain advised him to stop all communications with Persia and Russia and to never again receive their agents.

The First Anglo-Afghan War, 1839–1842

Dost Muhammad Khan rejected those British demands, and negotiations between Dost Muhammad and the British failed. The presence of the Russian envoy in Kabul convinced the British that the Afghan king was friendlier to the Russians than to them. Hence, fearful of a possible Russian advance toward India, the British invaded Afghanistan in 1839. The British justified the invasion by saying that in order to ensure the welfare of India they had to have a trustworthy ally as the ruler of Afghanistan.

Dost Muhammad Khan was king of Afghanistan until British forces invaded in 1839 and forced him into exile.

Frustrated with the British-appointed ruler Shah Shuja, citizens of Kabul rebelled in 1842 and killed three thousand British soldiers.

After several attacks, Dost Muhammad surrendered to the British and was sent into exile in India in the late 1840s. The British filled the royal vacancy with Shah Shuja, a former Afghan king who had been exiled to India. However, Afghans disliked the new king. He was considered a British pawn placed on the throne by force and with the help of *farangees* or non-Muslims— Hindus and Sikhs from India who comprised a large portion of Britain's invading army.

Dissatisfaction with the king and the British came to a head in January 1842, when the people of Kabul rebelled. In one of the most remarkable battles in both Afghan and British history, some three thousand British forces were killed and only 121 survived the retreat from Kabul. One survivor was William Brydon, a British officer on horseback, wounded on a dying horse. Although most Afghan historians usually cite him as the only survivor, in fact a few more British survived as prisoners and hostages. Shah Shuja was killed in the uprising, as were Alexander Burnes and Sir William Macnaghten, two principal architects of the First Anglo-Afghan War. Macnaghten's mutilated and headless body was displayed at the entrance to the Kabul bazaar by a mob. With the death of Shah Shuja and defeat of the British, Dost Muhammad Khan reascended the throne in 1842 and reigned until his death in 1863.

Thus the First Anglo-Afghan War failed to destroy Afghan independence. On the contrary, it dealt a blow to British prestige in the East. Dost Muhammad's policy toward both imperial powers changed after his return to the Afghan throne. According to author Abdul Samad Ghous, "[Dost Muhammad Khan] was by this time more experienced in British imperial ways and more aware of the geopolitically sensitive position of Afghanistan. He had undoubtedly concluded that it was in the best interest of his rule to refrain from any dealings with Russia."[2]

Stationary Policy

British policy toward Afghanistan also changed. After its defeat in the First Anglo-Afghan War, the British government temporarily abandoned the forward policy and replaced it with what was known as "stationary policy." The essence of this policy was noninterference in the affairs of Afghanistan. According to author Sayed S. Hussain, "[This policy] sought security [of India] in defensive posture, abhorred interference across the frontiers of India, and believed that expansion of Russia could best be checked through diplomacy and pressure in Europe than by physical confrontation in Afghanistan."[3] The British government contained its involvement in Afghan affairs to indirect means such as financial subsidies to the country's rulers. In return, Britain required Afghan leaders to resist Russian aggression. This new British strategy against Russian influence, British policy makers thought, would not only promote the independence of Afghanistan in its internal affairs but also increase the security of British India.

Russian Advances

Meanwhile, Russia took advantage of Britain's low-profile policy on Afghanistan and resumed its expansion in Central Asia. By 1843, Russian outposts had crept into parts of northern Afghanistan. The Russians also annexed most of the independent or semi-independent principalities of Central Asia including the Uzbekistan cities of Tashkent (the capital) annexed in 1865; Samarqand, annexed in 1868; Khiva, annexed in 1873; and Kokand, annexed in 1878.

In 1878 Russia dispatched a diplomatic mission to Kabul. The purpose of this mission was to secure the friendship of the Afghan ruler, Sher Ali Khan, Dost Muhammad Khan's son, as part of Russia's diplomatic offensive against Britain. Sher Ali tried to bar the mission from the country, but in the face of Russian insistence, Sher Ali gave in and reluctantly received the envoy in Kabul.

The British were worried—they were not convinced that Sher Ali would remain neutral and keep Afghanistan as a buffer zone. The British therefore dispatched its own mission to Afghanistan and warned the king, according to author Sayed S. Hussain, that "refusal to grant it a free passage and an honourable reception as has been accorded to the Russian mission will be considered as a hostile act."[4]

The British thought they had two choices to prevent Russia from taking over Afghanistan. They could negotiate a settlement with the Afghan king ensuring cooperation with only the British. If that did not work, they could destroy the Afghan kingdom and take over as much Afghan territory as was necessary to protect India from Russian advances. Sher Ali rejected this British ultimatum and threatened to fight the British if they invaded Afghanistan. The subsequent British invasion culminated in the Second Anglo-Afghan War of 1878–1880.

The Second Anglo-Afghan War, 1878–1880

A British force of forty thousand successfully invaded Afghanistan at three different points on November 21, 1878. During the war, Sher Ali's authority diminished considerably. Consequently, he left for Russia to seek its military assistance against Britain. Russia did not want to incite the British and therefore refused to offer Sher Ali support. He returned to Mazar-i-Sharif (a city in northern Afghanistan) where he died in 1879.

The British struck a deal with his son, Yakub, and appointed him Afghanistan's new ruler. In return, Yakub Khan signed the 1879 Treaty of Gandamak, which forced the government of Afghanistan to cede the border areas, notably the Khyber Pass (a thirty-three-mile-long parcel of land in the Safed Koh mountain range bordering Afghanistan and Pakistan) to the British. These areas, with their strategic military significance, eventually helped the British to defend India against the Russians. Yakub also accepted a permanent British mission to the country. He likewise agreed to permit the British to handle Afghanistan's foreign policy and to seek British approval before establishing diplomatic relations with any foreign country. In return the British gave the Afghan king financial support in the amount of several hundred thousands of Indian rupees annually and guaranteed the safety of Afghan borders against external aggression.

Realizing that, like Shah Shuja, Yakub was a British pawn, an Afghan military unit joined by a city mob revolted against both him and the British. This uprising led to the death of Sir Louis Cavagnari, the British political envoy at Yakub's court, and his

The British envoy in Afghanistan Sir Louis Cavagnari (center, seated) was killed during the 1879 revolt against the British and Afghanistan's ruler Yakub Khan.

staff. Yakub abdicated the throne and fled to India because he did not wish to share Shah Shuja's fate.

The Second Anglo-Afghan War thus proved more successful for the British than the first. They won control of Afghanistan's foreign policy, but Afghanistan retained full sovereignty in domestic affairs.

A Buffer State

After the British success in the Second Anglo-Afghan War, the new British government, formed in 1880, adopted a new policy that regarded Afghanistan as a buffer state. The new policy argued that a true defense of India was unattainable by competing with other powers in Central Asia. Instead, the British would concentrate on establishing a strong government in India, developing its resources, and perfecting the efficiency of its army.

The Russian leaders agreed that a continued military escalation of their rivalry with Britain in Central Asia was counterproductive. Consequently, they switched their policy to using diplomatic means in settling their differences. Therefore, the conflicting interests of two imperial powers did not permit either to establish itself in Afghanistan. The alternative to an armed clash over the territory was to transform Afghanistan into a state and use it as a buffer.

To implement this new strategy, the British searched for a new Afghan king and at the same time started demarcating Afganistan's borders. The British wanted a leader who would be favorable to their policies and acceptable to both the Afghans and the Russians. It was also in their interest to see that a strong ruler reigned over Afghanistan. They found these qualities in Abd ar-Rahman Khan, Dost Muhammad Khan's grandson. He had lived in exile in Russia for some twelve years prior to becoming the king. To choose him to be king was a daring move by the British because after living in Russia, Abd ar-Rahman Khan might be more loyal to Russians than British. However, his strong and charismatic personality and independent mind convinced the British to take the risk and support him as the new king of Afghanistan.

Abd ar-Rahman Khan assumed the throne in 1880 and maintained Afghanistan's neutrality. He did everything within his power to keep Russia and Britain at arm's length without giving either control of his country. The Afghan king had full sovereignty over the internal affairs of Afghanistan. With regard to Afghan foreign policy, Abd ar-Rahman Khan, like his predecessor, agreed to allow Britain to retain full control of Afghanistan's foreign relations in return for British financial support.

His reign became known as the reign of the "Iron" Abd ar-Rahman Khan because he consolidated the power of the central government and repressed the people of Afghanistan. Although Afghanistan had emerged as an entity in 1747, it was actually under Abd ar-Rahman Khan that its borders were established, its internal unification completed, and the modern concept of nationhood implanted.

Demarcation of Afghan Borders

In order for Afghanistan to be a successful buffer zone, its boundaries had to be acceptable to all competing interests in the area. During Abd ar-Rahman Khan's reign Britain and Russia participated through boundary commissions in drawing Afghanistan's borders. After an exchange of territory on the two sides of the Amu Dar'ya (Oxus River) was agreed to in 1893, the river became the natural boundary between Afghanistan and Russia. The boundaries between Iran and Afghanistan were fixed through British mediation in the 1870s.

The remaining problem was demarcation of the southern and eastern frontiers of Afghanistan with British India. Abd ar-Rahman Khan and Henry Mortimer Durand, foreign secretary of the government of India, signed the Durand Agreement in 1893. The agreement settled the boundaries between Afghanistan and British India, but it divided tribes and sometimes even villages along what was called the Durand Line.

From the Afghan point of view, the Durand Line had many disadvantages. It put a final end to any hopes of stretching Afghanistan's frontiers to the Indian Ocean. Thus, Afghanistan remained a landlocked country. The agreement also made the Afghan economy dependent on British India. According to re-

The Durand Line

The Durand Line marked the eastern and southern borders between Afghanistan and British India in 1893. It is named after Sir Henry Mortimer Durand, the foreign secretary of British India. The line was drawn as part of an agreement signed between Afghanistan and British India to make Afghanistan a buffer state between British India and czsarist Russia. This line divides eastern Pashtun tribes and their families. Some of them live in Pakistan, on the east side of the Durand Line, and the rest live in Afghanistan. The Afghan king signed the Durand Agreement under the assumption that the line was drawn and would remain in effect as long as Afghanistan remained a buffer state. However, when Pakistan separated from India, the Durand Line became the permanent border between Pakistan and Afghanistan. Afghanistan protested the permanency of the line on many occasions and accused Britain of intentionally using the line to divide eastern Pashtun tribes and their families.

scarcher Mohammad Daud Miraki, "Any subsequent initiative at independent development [by Afghans] met with retaliation from British India in the form of economic sanctions. These economic sanctions took the form of border closure between India and Afghanistan by the British."[5]

As a buffer state, Afghanistan was kept economically weak and politically isolated. The Afghan rulers were told that their existence and the fate of their country depended on London and St. Petersburg. Consequently, the Afghan kings were so preoccupied with the preservation of their throne and territorial integrity of their country that not enough time, money, or energy could be devoted to the economic and political development of the country. According to Professor Richard Newell, "Little permanent progress in establishing a state had been made in more than 120 years of effort. The swelling tides of European power and ambition made the prospects for the separate existence of Afghanistan increasingly dim."[6]

The War of Independence, 1919

Ultimately, the Afghans resented the continued British presence in their affairs and, during the reign of Amanullah Khan, put their imperial master to the test. Realizing that true independence meant casting off the British for good, Afghan forces attacked the British garrisons on May 3, 1919, initiating the war of independence (the Third Anglo-Afghan War).

Amanullah Khan's success won him independence from Britain and concluded the Great Game. On August 8, 1919, the British and Afghans signed the Treaty of Rawalpindi, in which Britain granted complete independence to Afghanistan in both domestic and foreign affairs.

The Afghan state owes its creation to colonial rivalry between British India and czarist Russia during the Great Game in the nineteenth century. The imperialistic ambitions of the two superpowers in Afghanistan retarded progress and development in the country. Afghanistan continued to maintain its geostrategic significance in the region and became a battleground of the Cold War in the middle of the twentieth century.

A New Game: The Cold War 2

After World War II British influence and power around the world declined, and the United States and the Soviet Union became the two dominant world powers. The United States advocated capitalism; the Soviet Union, communism—two very different ideologies. Communism embraces common ownership, uniformity, and atheism (disbelief in God). Capitalism, on the other hand, advocates free open markets, social diversity, and democracy. Eventually, as the two superpowers sought influence around the globe, their differences led them to engage in a competition that became known as the Cold War.

Although it was not a violent, or "hot" war, the Cold War brought animosity, distrust, tension, competition, and fear to nearly four decades of the twentieth century. It was during this period that Afghanistan regained its status as a pawn of superpowers, as the United States and the Soviet Union each manipulated military and foreign aid programs to try to sway the hearts and minds of Afghan people in its favor. This interest and interference in the country had drastic results that ultimately led to further disintegration of the Afghan state.

Soviet-American Economic Competition in Afghanistan

After the end of World War II, successive Afghan governments launched extensive long-range economic development projects designed to build the infrastructure of the economy and to improve its citizens' living standards. Lack of capital and technical know-how, however, was a major problem. Seeing that Afghanistan needed help, and each wanting to gain a foothold in the country, the United States and the Soviet Union each provided Afghanistan with massive amounts of aid that funded, among other things, hydroelectric power projects, the transit system, development of civil aviation, and education. According to author Barnett R. Rubin, "From 1955 to 1978 the Soviet Union provided Afghanistan with $1.7 billion in economic aid, while the United States furnished $533 million in economic aid."[7] The competition between the superpowers had an important impact on Afghanistan's development.

To develop and modernize Afghanistan, the United States undertook the Helmand Valley Project. The purpose of this project was to provide hydroelectric power and to develop the arid Helmand Valley area, located in the southern part of Afghanistan. The Soviet Union also helped Afghanistan with the construction of hydroelectric power stations and land reclamation projects in several parts of the country. One of these projects, the Nangarhar Valley Project, was built in eastern Afghanistan. It leveled some twenty-three thousand acres of land and established four state farms, which produced citrus fruits and olives.

Experts from the U.S. Army Corps of Engineers were used to direct the construction of the Kabul-Kandahar section of the main highway, with spurs leading to the Afghan-Pakistan border at Spin Baldak, southeast of Kandahar. The Soviet Union also constructed highways in the northern and western parts of the country that connected with those built by the United States in the east and south. One of these Soviet-constructed highways links Kabul to the port of Sher Khan Bandar, on a former Afghan-Soviet border. Located along this road is Salang Pass, a nearly two-mile-long tunnel that passes over the Hindu Kush at an altitude of about ten thousand feet above sea level.

Both superpowers also helped to develop Afghanistan's aviation industry. The Afghan Air Authority was organized with the help of the U.S. Federal Aviation Administration. Pan American Airways, a former American airline company, helped to establish the Afghan national airline. For their part, the Soviets provided help in the construction of the Kabul airport, the

Bagram military airport, and several smaller ones around the country.

Education was another area that received Soviet-American aid. The education, agriculture, and engineering colleges of Kabul University came to depend primarily upon American aid for their laboratory equipment and professional staff. Moreover, grants were made available for Afghan students to attend

The arid Helmand Valley is located in southern Afghanistan. To develop the area, the United States funded a project that provided hydroelectric power.

American universities. An important Soviet contribution to education was the construction of the Polytechnic Institute on the campus of Kabul University. This Soviet-sponsored higher-education institution offered courses in geology and exploration for mineral deposits and exploitation of oil and gas fields, among others.

Economic Legacy of the New Game

Although for years various Afghan governments took advantage of the new game by pitting the two superpowers against each other for economic benefits, Afghanistan ultimately became the victim of foreign aid. Sole reliance on the United States and the Soviet Union for economic aid created economic dependency, which crippled the country. Since most goods and services were provided from outside the country, Afghans were not encouraged to domestically deliver or produce them. As a result, citizens had no source of income. Therefore, foreign aid was the major source of income because the Afghan governments did not have any major sources of taxes to generate money for government-sponsored programs.

Moreover, while the United States and the Soviet Union financed these various projects, they also supervised and completed them. This practice produced an absence of badly needed Afghan professionals for future long-term development. Because such professionals came from outside the country, Afghan citizens did not become engineers or doctors or lawyers—they relied on the superpowers to provide these professionals for them. Researcher Mohammed Daud Miraki observes, "Due to the excessive reliance on the donors for supervision and lack of commitment on the part of Afghan officials, development resources [such as home-grown professionals] were mismanaged and wasted."[8] The development of Afghanistan was further stifled because it was determined and limited to a certain extent by the need of the superpowers. For example, most of the yields of the Nangarhar Valley Project, citrus fruits and olives, were sent to the Soviet Union because they could not be produced in the Soviet Union. Most of these products were not found at local markets in Afghanistan for domestic consumption.

The Competition Bears Arms

Afghanistan was also in dire need of modernizing its armed forces, and Afghanistan armed forces came to depend heavily on the Soviets for military equipment and training.

The Afghan government decided to mobilize its armed forces to accomplish three main goals: to maintain internal security, to gain control over powerful and fiercely independent tribes, and to strengthen the central government to foster political and economic development. The Afghan government first approached the United States for such help and made several requests for U.S. arms aid between 1953 and 1955.

The U.S. government, however, turned down the Afghan requests for several reasons. First, the Afghan government's refusal to join the American-sponsored military alliance, the 1955 Baghdad Pact, was perceived by the United States as an unfriendly gesture. Moreover, the United States feared such arms might be used against its ally Pakistan, which was engaged in a territorial dispute with Afghanistan over the Durand Line.

In 1956, after Afghanistan's request for U.S. military aid proved fruitless, Afghanistan turned to its northern neighbor, the Soviet Union, to modernize the Afghan armed forces. Seeing a ripe opportunity to gain influence, the Soviet Union immediately granted the request. The military deliveries initially consisted of obsolete weapons and small arms. But by the early 1960s the Soviets were supplying Afghan armed forces with sophisticated aircraft, such as MiG-21s, along with other new weapons, including SA-2 missiles and modern T-54 tanks. Soviet instructors and maintenance experts accompanied the aircraft and other weapons. Researcher Riffat Sardar observes that, "By 1977, the Soviet Union had supplied more than 700 tanks [such as] T-3s, T-54/55s and T-62s, and 184 combat aircraft [such as] MiG-17s, MiG-21s, Il-28s and SU-7s."[9] Furthermore, the Soviets built military airfields in Bagram, near Kabul, at Mazar-i-Sharif in northern Afghanistan, and at Shindand in the central part of western Afghanistan.

*Afghan soldiers undergo weapons training. The Soviet Union
contributed millions of dollars to modernize Afghanistan's military.*

Meanwhile, the Afghans sent their pilot trainees and military personnel to the Soviet Union for schooling and technical training in the use and operation of the new equipment. According to researcher Muhammad Azmi, "By 1977, . . . the Afghan army's strength had risen to 100,000 officers . . . thanks to an estimated $600 million worth of military and assistance from the USSR."[10]

While in the Soviet Union for military training, the Afghan students were required to take courses in Communist ideology and Marxism-Leninism. Some even married Russians while they were there. Upon their return home the newly Soviet-trained Afghan military officers either joined the Afghan Communist Party or became sympathetic to it.

Origin of the Communist Party in Afghanistan

Afghanistan's Communist Party, the People's Democratic Party of Afghanistan (PDPA), was founded in January 1965. After just two years of its existence, however, the PDPA split into two groups and remained divided until July 1977. One faction of the PDPA was called Parcham (meaning banner) with an officer named Babrak Karmal as its leader. The other faction called itself Khalq (meaning masses), with an officer named Noor Mohammed Taraki as its leader. Each claimed to be the true PDPA. The rift occurred as a result of personal ambitions as well as ethnic and policy differences.

In 1973 the Parcham helped Muhammad Daud Khan, a former prime minister, oust King Muhammad Zahir Shah from power in a bloodless coup. Daud declared himself the president of Afghanistan and originally included members of Parcham in his government. Once Daud consolidated his power, however, he marginalized the role of the Parcham and later dismissed them from his government. Daud also tried to increase the role of major oil-producing Islamic countries, including Iran, Kuwait, and Saudi Arabia, in the economic development of Afghanistan at the expense of the Soviet Union.

The Soviets concluded that Daud had become too independent to be tolerated. Both his domestic and foreign policies seemed to run against Moscow's wishes. They were instead designed, the Soviets concluded, to reduce dependence on the Soviet Union and to draw Afghanistan closer to the United States.

The Saur Revolution

Around this time the two Communist factions were reunited, and in July 1977 once more became known as the PDPA. Then, in early April 1978, Mir Akbar Khyber, a prominent leader of the Parcham, was assassinated. The PDPA leadership pointed the finger at President Daud, accusing him of being involved in the assassination. Khyber's murder set in motion a series of events that led to a coup d'état. On April 27, 1978, the Soviet-trained Afghan

Muhammad Daud Khan

Muhammad Daud Khan was born in 1919. He served in different cabinet posts throughout the 1940s before King Muhammad Zahir, his cousin, appointed him prime minister in 1953. As prime minister he played a major role in social reform and modernization of Afghan society. He was the first public official to encourage Afghan women to appear in public unveiled.

In an effort to consolidate his power, King Muhammad Zahir forced Daud Khan to resign in 1963. After ten years of private life, Daud Khan staged a coup against the king and abolished the monarchy in 1973. He relied on the support of the Parcham faction of the People's Democratic Party of Afghanistan to acquire and unify his regime. He later became disillusioned by the Parcham's role in his government and dismissed them.

When Muhammad Daud Khan attempted to improve relations with the West in order to reduce the Soviet influence in Afghanistan, he and members of his family were assassinated by the leaders of the pro-Soviet coup in 1978.

Daud Khan led the 1973 uprising that abolished the monarchy. He was assassinated in 1978.

military officers, led by Colonel Abdul Qader, staged a bloody and successful coup d'état on behalf of the PDPA and seized power. It is not known what direct role the Soviet Union played, but the coup engineers had the Soviets' approval. When President Daud refused to surrender, the coup leaders executed him and most members of his family.

The coup d'état became known as the Saur Revolution ("Saur" is the word for April in the Afghan language). Immediately after seizing power, the Soviet Union recognized the new Communist government of Afghanistan, which renamed the country the Democratic Republic of Afghanistan. As hoped, the Soviets won a Communist ally in Afghanistan, a new player on their Cold War team. The PDPA signed a treaty with the Soviet Union on December 3, 1978, which said, among other things, that both sides would consult with each other and take appropriate measures to ensure the security, independence, and territorial integrity of the two countries.

Once they assumed power, however, the unity that the Afghan Communists had briefly enjoyed broke down. Old rivalry and feuding quickly resurfaced, and the PDPA dissolved again into the two groups, the Khalq and Parcham. Noor Mohammed Taraki, leader of the Khalq, became the prime minister of Afghanistan and Babrak Karmal, the leader of the Parcham, became the senior deputy prime minister. Hafizullah Amin, another leader of the Khalq and a future president, was named foreign minister.

Several months after the coup d'état, members of Khalq began orchestrating ways to rid the government of their Parcham opponents. Several prominent leaders, such as Karmal, were dismissed from their government posts and appointed to ambassadorial positions abroad. Other members of the Parcham were either fired from their government posts, arrested, forced underground, or executed.

Rivalry Within the Khalq

Even after the Parcham was eliminated, intense rivalry and a power struggle ensued between the two leaders of the Khalq, Taraki and Amin. Each wanted to head the government. Amin gained control of army and security forces. In mid-September 1979 there was a shoot-out between the aides of Amin and Taraki inside the presidential palace, renamed the People's House. Anthony Arnold observes, "As [Amin and his bodyguards] entered the building, they fell into an ambush, and at least four of the escorts, including Taroon [Amin's personal bodyguard], were killed. Amin, however, fought his way clear and survived unscathed."[11] Following the palace shoot-out, Taraki was arrested and strangled on Amin's orders. Now controlled by Amin, the media, which used to hail Taraki as the "great teacher, great genius, and great leader," announced that he had died of a "serious illness"[12] on October 9, 1979.

After getting rid of his opponents inside the PDPA, Amin instituted a program of radical socialism and brutal oppression. The Amin secret police arrested and executed tens of thousands of people who were considered to be a potential threat to Amin's regime. Those targeted included intellectuals, educated elite, high school and college students, and religious and opposition political leaders.

The Revolutionary Council of the PDPA between May and November 1978 introduced social and economic reforms in the form of decrees. Among the social reforms was the introduction of the new national flag. The traditional Islamic green flag was replaced by a blood red one, a close copy of the Soviet flag. The Communist government also initiated a land reform program that limited maximum land ownership by a family to 14.3 acres of land. The rest of the privately owned lands were confiscated and redistributed to the landless peasants. Social changes included reducing bride-prices and prohibiting arranged marriages.

Most of these reforms challenged prevailing traditional and Islamic values and the sentiments of the population and thus encountered bitter resistance throughout the country, especially from the rural population. Some people expressed their opposition to these reforms by leaving the country. Others refused to comply with these reform programs. Still others picked up arms against the government. In March 1979 there was a major uprising in Herat, a city near the Iranian border. This military uprising was led by Captain Ismail Khan, who took over the city for several days before he was pushed back by government forces. Many Soviet advisers, their families, and government soldiers were killed in this uprising. Similar spontaneous uprisings took place in other parts of the country.

The Soviet Occupation

Although President Amin was a Communist ally, the Soviet Union was becoming very alarmed at the unstable, unpredictable situation on its southern border. By 1979 the Amin government was on the verge of collapse, and the Soviets doubted he could control the country for much longer. They also feared that radical fundamental Islam growing inside of Afghanistan could take over as the prevailing ideology, as it had during the Islamic revolution in Iran that same year.

The Soviet Union invaded Afghanistan in December 1979. Afghans resented the presence of Russian soldiers and formed a resistance movement.

Babrak Karmal

Babrak Karmal was born in 1929 in a village outside of Kabul. His father was a general in the army and also served as a governor when Muhammad Zahir was king. He was admitted to the faculty of law and political science at Kabul University in 1951. Due to his political activism and stimulation of student unrest at the university, Karmal was imprisoned in 1952. After completing his term in jail, Karmal returned to the university and graduated. He became a full-time politician in 1964. He also became a regular visitor to the Soviet embassy in Kabul where he received political instructions and personal favors from the Soviet KGB.

He helped establish the People's Democratic Party of Afghanistan in 1965. After eighteen months of exile in Moscow, Karmal was installed as president when the Soviet Union invaded Afghanistan. After his unsuccessful attempt to unify the country, he was deposed from power by the Soviet Union in 1986 and lived in exile in Moscow until he died in December 1996.

Afghanistan had also become an increasingly attractive economic and geopolitical resource to the Soviets, due to its proximity to Middle East oil reserves. The Soviet military was also gaining strength and wanted to directly experiment with its armed forces. The Soviets wanted to expose their units to real-life combat conditions and experience, and they believed that Afghanistan would be an ideal setting for that experience.

Taking into account all of these factors, the Kremlin decided to use force to overthrow Amin and his regime. On December 25, 1979, some 115,000 Soviet troops invaded Afghanistan. Amin was toppled and murdered. Little is known how about he died, but some speculate that he was killed by a special Soviet commando unit while he was entertaining his guests at the opening of the new presidential palace in the outskirts of the capital. The USSR installed a new PDPA regime headed by ex-Parcham leader Babrak Karmal, who was brought into the country from exile by Soviet paratroopers during the invasion.

The pervasive Soviet presence in Afghanistan alienated wide segments of the population. Soviet soldiers patrolled the streets of Kabul and other major cities. They swept through villages, leaving mines in mosques and in the fields, some disguised as toys, that would kill civilians, especially curious children, when they tried to pick them up.

Although Babrak Karmal was formally in charge of the country, in reality the Soviets were in control. They dominated the bureaucracy by acting as military and civilian advisers to different governmental departments. Karmal, who ruled from 1980 to 1986, attempted to undo the Khalq's reform programs in order to win the support of the people. For example, he actively used Islam as a source of legitimacy for his regime by restoring the traditional Islamic colors of the Afghan flag and invoking the name of God before delivering his speeches to the nation. His government also announced that it would postpone the implementation of the Communist land reform program.

But Afghans viewed Karmal as merely a Soviet puppet and refused to grant his regime legitimacy. Instead, they resorted to continued resistance and violence against the Soviet occupation and the Karmal regime. Others fled to Pakistan and Iran and organized resistance groups against the government.

Resistance Movement

Organized resistance to the Soviet occupation took the form of a religious jihad or holy war—a war in defense of Islam against the atheist regime of Kabul. Those who fought on behalf of Islam became known as the mujahideen (freedom fighters). They became the heart of the organized resistance against the Soviet occupation. Their struggle was waged to free Afghanistan from communism and restore an Islamic government. They established their headquarters and bases in Peshawar, Pakistan, and were made up of seven military-political organizations (*tanzims*).

The United States condemned the Soviet invasion and considered it a threat to the rest of the region, especially the oil-producing states of the Middle East. The United States was also concerned about the spread of communism and the growing influence of the Soviet Union. In order to contain further Soviet expansion, the United States began to support the opposition in Afghanistan.

American president Ronald Reagan considered the situation in Afghanistan to be a valuable political opportunity in America's global conflict with the Soviet Union. He wanted to support the mujahideen in order to bog down the Soviet Union in a protracted conflict that would drain them of their resources and ultimately weaken them. In his State of the Union message before the members of Congress in February 1985, Reagan stated that America must support those who defied Soviet-supported aggression. He further stated that support for freedom fighters was self-defense for America.

This statement became known as the Reagan Doctrine. The purpose of the doctrine was to help free nations under Communist domination. To implement this doctrine in Afghanistan, Reagan signed the National Security Decision Directive 66, which called for American efforts to drive Soviet forces from Afghanistan by all means available.

The CIA and the Arab Afghans

The Central Intelligence Agency (CIA) was provided with several billion dollars to launch the largest covert operation it had ever undertaken. The goal was to help the mujahideen defeat communism in Afghanistan during the 1980s. The CIA also placed advertisements in newspapers and newsletters in the Arab countries motivating young Muslims to join the Afghan "holy war."

Those who answered these advertisements became known as the Arab Afghans. According to author Mark Huband, "At [the campaign's] height there were around fifteen thousand who came from Saudi Arabia, five thousand from Yemen, between three and five thousand from Egypt, two thousand from Algeria, around one thousand from the Gulf, a thousand from Libya, and several hundred from Iraqi Kurdistan." [13] The most famous of these Arab Afghans was Osama bin Laden, who joined the mujahideen in 1986.

Until 1986 the Americans were careful not to supply the fighters with U.S.-made arms. The strategy was to minimize the appearance of American involvement in the early stage of the war against the Soviet occupying force. The CIA counterinsurgency experts, therefore, purchased Soviet-made weapons from Egypt, China, India, and Israel. The CIA used the Pakistani military intelligence service, Inter-Services Intelligence (ISI), to organize the resistance groups and supply them with arms. The ISI allocated the weapons among the seven Peshawar-based organizations, who in turn distributed them inside Afghanistan to local commanders.

When the ugly details of the Soviet occupation of Afghanistan became known worldwide, the United States decided that it was time to openly and directly support the opposition. Therefore, the United States supplied the mujahideen with American arms,

Members of the mujahideen rejoice after capturing a Russian personnel carrier during the war against Soviet occupation.

including the shoulder-held, laser-guided, heat-seeking Stinger missiles. The Stinger missiles inflicted many casualties as they destroyed hundreds of government aircraft and helicopters.

The war in Afghanistan drained the Soviet Union of both its material and human resources. It cost the Soviet Union tens of billions of dollars and the lives of over fifteen thousand Soviet soldiers. The Kremlin leaders had failed in their efforts to consolidate the Communist regime in Afghanistan and realized their blunder in 1986 when Mikhail Gorbachev called Afghanistan "a bleeding wound." [14] Eventually the Soviet Union was forced to sign the United Nations–sponsored Geneva Accords in April 1988. The signatories to the accords included the Afghan government, the Soviet Union, Pakistan, and the United States. Specifically, the accords required the Soviet Union to withdraw all its forces from Afghanistan by February 1989. The last Afghan Communist government and its leader, Najibullah Ahmedzai, continued to rule in the absence of the Soviet forces until 1992.

The mujahideen were not invited to the Geneva negotiations because the Geneva Accords dealt with the Soviet withdrawal and not the composition of the future government in Afghanistan. The mujahideen rejected the Geneva Accords and continued their resistance against the last Soviet-sponsored government of Ahmedzai. By early 1992, due to lack of continued Russian military and economic support, the last Communist government collapsed. The mujahideen assumed power and declared the Islamic State of Afghanistan. The mujahideen agreed to create a broad-based temporary government and hold general elections within two years.

A Crumbled Unity

However, the mujahideen could not agree among themselves over the sharing of power and soon turned their guns against each other. As fighting among various groups of mujahideen escalated, Afghanistan became engulfed in civil war and was divided into several independent zones, each with its own warlord.

The civil war lasted for four years and had devastating consequences for the country. The capital was divided into zones

As a result of the Geneva Accords, the Soviet military was required to withdraw from Afghanistan in February 1989.

of occupation, where competing factions of mujahideen occupied different parts of the city. The power struggle over the control of Kabul turned the city into armed camps. More than twenty-five thousand civilians lost their lives in Kabul alone. Government buildings, schools, mosques, and residential areas were utterly destroyed and Kabul was reduced to rubble.

There was a shortage of food, electricity, and water. The battle for control of Kabul was a microcosm of what took place all over Afghanistan. Afghanistan's cities, which had been spared earlier destruction during the Soviet occupation, became the targets of the civil war. The country immersed itself in ethnic and religious violence, which led to further political fragmentation of Afghanistan.

Thus, the new game played between the United States and the Soviet Union in Afghanistan brought death and utter destruction to the country. During the civil war many Afghans lost their lives and several million Afghans abandoned their homes and went into exile in neighboring countries, mainly Pakistan and Iran. Major cities were completely destroyed. Although the mujahideen had recaptured their country from a major superpower and saved it from a dominant world ideology, they could not set aside their religious and ethnic differences and work toward a unified national government. As a result, the Afghan state once again collapsed.

The Taliban: From Chaos to Clampdown 3

Civil war raged in Afghanistan until 1996, when a group called the Taliban captured Kabul from warring factions of mujahideen. Their rule marked a change from chaotic civil war to a tightly controlled, brutally suppressive regime. The Taliban were the embodiment of religious ultraconservatism and enforced a rigid theocracy, or governance according to religious doctrine. Their draconian rule effectively alienated Afghanistan from the rest of the world, except Pakistan, Saudi Arabia, and the United Arab Emirates—the three countries that recognized the Taliban regime until its demise. The Taliban also provided sanctuary for Osama bin Laden (a dissident ex–Saudi Arabian citizen now in hiding), his al-Qaeda network, and his extreme Islamic supporters who used Afghanistan as a training ground for terrorism abroad.

Origin of the Taliban

The word Taliban is derived form the Arabic word *talib*. A *talib* is an Islamic student, one who seeks knowledge before he becomes a mullah or a pastor in a mosque. Journalist Ahmed Rashid observes that, "As most of them [the Taliban] were part-time or full-time students at *madrasas* [Islamic seminary schools], the name they chose for themselves was natural." [15] Most members of the Taliban lived as refugees in Pakistan during the 1979–1989 Soviet occupation of Afghanistan. They attended the *madrasa* in Northeast Frontier Province and Baluchistan Province in Pakistan.

Mullah Mohammad Omar, an Afghan Pashtun, became the Taliban movement's leader in the southern city of Kandahar in Afghanistan. He fought against the Soviets during their occupation of Afghanistan and lost an eye during one of the battles. His bravery, charismatic personality, leadership in the battlefield, and his commitment to and knowledge of Islam earned him respect and prestige among his fellow Taliban. Following the Soviet withdrawal in 1989, Omar returned to his village of Sangasar in Kandahar Province where he became a mullah at a local mosque.

After the mujahideen captured Kabul in April 1992, most mujahideen became warlords and began fighting among themselves for control. Professor Peter Marsden observes,

> After . . . 1992, the Afghan people thought that peace would prevail in the country. However, the leaders began to fight over power in Kabul. Some local leaders, particularly in Qandahar, formed gangs that fought each other. There was widespread corruption and theft, and there were roadblocks everywhere. Women were being attacked, raped and killed. Therefore, after these incidents, a group of students from religious schools decided to rise against these leaders in order to alleviate the suffering of the residence of Qandahar Province. [16]

It was in the backdrop to this chaotic situation that the Taliban originated. Omar founded the Taliban movement to fight corruption and lawlessness, to end the civil war, and to create a pure Islamic society.

The Rise of the Taliban

The Taliban first became active in October 1994, when Afghan bandits hijacked a convoy of Pakistani trucks in Kandahar. Several hundred Taliban arrived, freed the convoy, and, after four days of fighting, captured Kandahar on November 5, 1994. Meanwhile, thousands of young Afghan Pashtuns, who had been studying in different Pakistani *madrasas,* rushed to Kandahar to join the Taliban movement. They were attracted to the Taliban's view of establishing a pure Islamic regime. Pakistani volunteers from the same religious schools and the Arab Afghans (Arabs who came to fight the Soviets in Afghanistan alongside the Afghan mujahideen) who were inspired by the new Islamic movement also joined. By December 1994, some twelve thousand Afghan and Pakistani students had joined the Taliban.

Mujahideen ride in the trunk of a car in Kabul. After the Soviet withdrawal, most mujahideen became warlords and began fighting among themselves.

The Taliban continued their advances, and by February 11, 1995, they controlled nine of Afghanistan's thirty-two provinces. On September 5, 1995, the Taliban seized Herat, a major city in the northwest. Just over one year later Jalalabad, a major city in the east, fell, and fifteen days later, on September 26, 1996, the Taliban took Kabul. The Afghan president Burhanuddin Rabbani escaped to the north, where he later formed the Northern Alliance. The next day, the Taliban assassinated Najibullah Ahmedzai, the last Soviet-sponsored president who lived under house arrest in the offices of the United Nations in Kabul. They hanged his body from a traffic platform in a public square to demonstrate a total rejection of Soviet rule and Communist ideology. His execution was the first symbolic, brutal act by the Taliban in Kabul.

On May 24, 1997, the Taliban seized Mazar-i-Sharif, the last major city held by the mujahideen. However, after eighteen hours a rebellion broke out and forced the Taliban to leave the city. A year later, though, the Taliban reentered Mazar-i-Sharif and took control of the city. With the capture of Mazar-i-Sharif, the Taliban held nearly 90 percent of the Afghan territory.

The Taliban instituted a political system based on the system of caliphs, or successors, who succeeded the prophet Muhammad. Emulating the early caliphate, the Taliban created a Supreme Council (*Majlis-i-Shura*) consisting of twenty individuals, whose members chose Omar as the Taliban's leader. He was named the *Amir ul-Momineen,* or commander of the faith, both for his proven political and military strength during the Soviet occupation and for his piety and unswerving belief in Islam. The country was renamed the Islamic Emirate of Afghanistan.

The Taliban Achievement

Because the people of Afghanistan had suffered tremendously from infighting among the warlords, the arrival of the Taliban was initially welcomed and celebrated in Kabul in September 1996. During their six years in power, the Taliban succeeded in ending anarchy and in bringing relative peace and security to a lawless and chaotic nation. They banished all warlords by forcing them to move to the northeastern corner of the country (where they formed the Northern Alliance and continued to oppose the Taliban). The Taliban disarmed most of the population and unified 90 percent of the country under their leadership. Although the remaining 10 percent stayed under the control of the Northern Alliance, they did not threaten the Taliban's grip on the majority of the country.

The Taliban soon proved they had their own brand of justice. While it was true they restored law and order, they did so through rigorous enforcement of Islamic punishment such as public beating, flogging, amputation of hands, and stoning or shooting to death. As a result of such harsh punishments the Taliban got rid of thieves, gangs, highway robbers, and corruption. Most residents of Kabul felt so safe that they did not object to the brutal punishments. Leila Helms, an Afghan American who lobbied on behalf of the Taliban before Congress, commented, "I am helping them [the Taliban] because they are doing the right thing for the country. They have brought peace and security, law and order, things that the country [is] incredibly in need of." [17] Researcher Barnett R. Rubin further explains why the Taliban's methods were seen as a positive contribution to the country: "The Taliban takeover of Kabul had one positive humanitarian consequence

The Northern Alliance, a movement that resisted the Taliban, emerged soon after the Taliban seized power. Armed with a machine gun, this twelve-year-old boy is ready to join the resistance.

in the city: it ended the blockade of Kabul, with the result that both food and other items of trade could reach it more easily." [18]

The Taliban Clampdown

Soon, however, the Taliban set about clamping down on the entire character of the country. One of the powerful arms of the Taliban movement was the Ministry for the Promotion of Virtue and Suppression of Vice. This ministry issued strict religious decrees and informed the general public of new rules through the Taliban radio station, Radio Shariat. Over time, decrees were passed that denied people the right to freedom of expression, association, the right to work, and the right to education.

The Taliban regime issued rigid decrees that were enforced by agents like this one who patrolled the streets. Violators were punished severely.

The Ministry for the Promotion of Virtue and Suppression of Vice was one of the most dreaded of the Taliban's political institutions. Most Afghans associated it with the word *wahshat* or "terror." The ministry was made up of religious police who were responsible for enforcement of all Taliban decrees regarding moral behavior. They enforced rules on such matters as the appearance of women, dress, employment, medical care, behavior, religious practice, and freedom of expression.

The agents of this ministry were young zealots, who walked around with whips, long sticks, and Kalashnikov machine guns. They constantly roamed the streets, shops, and hospitals to make sure people adhered to the moral code of behavior. They were also on the lookout for people conspiring against the Taliban regime and were empowered to jail any person who looked suspicious or was considered to be in violation of specific decrees.

A series of decrees covered appearance, and the specifications were derived from strict interpretation of rules set forth in the Koran. For example, the Taliban argued that, in the tradition of the prophet Muhammad and his followers, men must wear a long beard. Therefore, the Taliban forbade men to shave, and police could jail a man for not wearing a beard at least the length of one fist. Men would often be kept in detention centers for several months until their beards grew to at least the required length.

Other restrictions were put in place regarding clothing and appearance. Men were ordered to wear a turban and refrain from Western haircuts or dress. Women were forbidden to wear lipstick, necklaces, and high-heeled shoes, as these items were considered un-Islamic. The Taliban claimed they were safeguarding women and their honor and dignity.

The Taliban passed another series of decrees denying Afghans access to entertainment. They prohibited games, music, cassette tapes, kite flying, chess, and the pastime of domesticating pigeons, claiming that these activities took time away from one's religious duties and practices. The Taliban forbade the people to watch television, and they also closed the cinemas. (The buildings were converted into mosques.)

Religious Persecution

The Taliban took specific steps to assure the purity and pervasiveness of Islam in Afghanistan. One way in which they did this was by punishing anyone who converted away from Islam. Conversion from Islam was considered apostasy and was punishable by instant death. In early August 2001 the Taliban arrested some members of Shelter Now, an international relief agency with multinational employees. They threatened to execute the agency's Afghan employees for allegedly converting to Christianity from Islam.

The Taliban also singled out the Hindus who had lived in Afghanistan for many years, privately practicing their religion. A decree was issued requiring that all Hindus wear a yellow badge to distinguish them from Muslims. People equated this action to Nazi Germany, where Jews were required to wear badges identifying them as Jews. The Taliban justified their action by arguing that wearing a yellow badge was an effort to safeguard Hindus from mistreatment and harassment by the religious police. However, it served to religiously segregate them and make them obvious victims of persecution.

The Taliban also viewed the presence of centuries-old Afghan statues and paintings as un-Islamic idols and ordered them to be destroyed. Following the capture of the western city of Herat, the Taliban ordered the work of a well-known Herati artist destroyed immediately, claiming it was heretical. According to the *World Press Review,* "Muhammad Saeed Mashal, one of Afghanistan's most respected artists, had been painting a grand tableau on the walls of the main reception hall at the governor's office, depicting 400 years of Herat's achievements in art, architecture, science, and letters. The intricate murals were just a few months from completion [when the Taliban ordered them] to be whitewashed."[19] They also ordered the destruction of two large second-century statues of the Buddha carved in a cliff in the central province of Bamian. They were considered among the world's great cultural treasures, but the Taliban considered them affronts to Islam.

Destruction of Buddha Statues

Before Islam came to Afghanistan, most Afghans were under Buddhist influence. Buddhism was introduced to Afghanistan during the Kushan Empire, which existed from the second century B.C. to the third century A.D. Among the best known of the Kushan rulers was Kanishka, who established a summer capital at Kapisa, north of Kabul. It was during his reign that Buddhism reached its height in the region. As a tribute to Buddhism, Kanishka had two huge statues of Buddha carved into the red sandstone cliffs in Bamian in central Afghanistan. The larger towered over 175 feet high. The statues were among Asia's great archaeological treasures, and Bamian was an important place of pilgrimage.

The Taliban saw the ancient Buddha statues at Bamian as an affront to Islam and issued a decree to destroy them in 2001.

The statues survived until the Taliban's supreme leader, Mullah Mohammad Omar, issued a decree to destroy them. The destruction of statues was part of a campaign by the Taliban regime to rid Afghanistan of all un-Islamic graven images. Despite worldwide condemnation of the decree, Mullah Omar's order was carried out and the statues were reduced to a heap of rubble in March 2001.

An Islamic Emirate

The Taliban required all Afghans to take part in five daily prayers. New mosques were built all over the cities with loudspeakers on top of their roofs so that people could hear and respond to the call for prayer. Shopkeepers were required to close their stores during prayer times and attend mosque. Those who failed to attend mosque during prayer time were reprimanded by the religious soldiers and escorted to the mosque to perform their prayers. After morning prayers most mosques were converted into schools where young boys took Islamic lessons from the mullah of the mosque. Religious education was the only education boys were allowed to receive.

Under the Taliban regime, education received a major blow, as all female teachers were officially prohibited from teaching and girls' schools were shut down. Girls, up to eight years of age, were permitted to attend only *madrasas,* where they were trained in Islamic law and taught how to read the Koran. Girls were denied any further education after they finished at the *madrasas.*

The Taliban denial of educational opportunities for girls and women brought wide condemnation around the world. Amnesty International, a London-based human rights organization, called Afghanistan under the Taliban "a human rights catastrophe." [20] The Taliban argued that lack of adequate security in the country made it unsafe for girls to attend schools and promised to reopen them when the situation improved.

Moreover, they maintained that the decrees were issued in accordance to *Shari'a,* Islamic law. Critics of the Taliban, however, argued that the Taliban's idea of Islam was a gross misrepresentation of religion. Ziaba Shorish-Shamly, an Afghan American activist, made the following observation about the Taliban: "Islam granted men and women equal rights in the 6th century. But Islam has become the hostage of fanatic groups, such as the Taliban, whose misguided interpretation of Islam, combined with their tribal laws and customs, have made the [people] of Afghanistan virtual prisoners in their own society." [21]

Because the Taliban regime was mainly preoccupied with the religious and moral aspects of Afghan society, they ignored the economic state of the country. As a result, people became engulfed in poverty. Saira Shah, a British journalist of Afghan descent observes, "My hosts . . . used to live middle-class lives. The father trained as an engineer but nobody is building the country's shattered infrastructure, so he ekes out a living tailoring. I was woken every morning at 3 A.M., when the electricity came on. The whole family worked frantically at the sewing machines until it went out again at 5 A.M. All day they toiled to find clean water, and food they could not afford in the market." [22]

World Reaction

Among 190 members of the United Nations, only Pakistan, Saudi Arabia, and the United Arab Emirates (UAE) recognized the Taliban government. Pakistan supported and recognized the regime for both political and economic reasons. As Afghanistan's next-door neighbor, Pakistan was comfortable with the stability the Taliban had ushered into Afghanistan. In addition, Pakistan wanted to open a trade route through Afghanistan, and saw the stable Afghanistan as in its best economic interest. The Saudis and UAE supported the Taliban government because they felt affinity to the Taliban view and to the practice of Islam. The rest of the world, however, outraged at the Taliban's illegal seizure of power and draconian rule, refused to recognize them.

Initially, the United States gave lukewarm support to the Taliban. Although they did not diplomatically recognize them, they hoped the regime would be a partner in oil-pipeline construction through the region. However, it soon became apparent that the Taliban were not receptive to business. When it became clear that the fundamentalist regime was committing grave human rights abuses, the United States pulled out all support.

Human Rights Watch, Amnesty International, and various women's organizations around the world soon condemned the Taliban's suppression of human rights and their Islamic fundamentalist agenda. They accused the Taliban of total disregard for human rights and of serious crimes against humanity. They also viewed the Taliban's cruel, inhuman, and degrading methods of punishment to be in violation of international norms of behavior.

Harboring an Enemy

In addition to committing human rights abuses, the Taliban also harbored terrorists and had granted refuge to one of the world's most dangerous people, Osama bin Laden. Bin Laden has been linked to nearly every Islamic fundamentalist act of terrorism in the past decade, from the 1993 bombing of the World Trade Center, to the 1996 bombing of the Khobar Towers (a U.S. military installation in Saudi Arabia), to the 1998 bombing of two American embassies in East Africa.

Bin Laden was born into a wealthy family in Saudi Arabia in 1957 and was twenty-two when he decided to come to Afghanistan to both finance and fight alongside Afghans in their jihad against the Soviets. Bin Laden's political views were shaped while fighting with the mujahideen. The defeat of the Soviet Union was an inspiration for him. It radicalized him and he emerged from the war as a leader.

He established an organization known as al-Qaeda (the base) in the late 1980s when he moved to Afghanistan. Its original purpose was to bring together Arabs who fought in Afghanistan against the Soviet Union to continue the jihad worldwide. Specifically, it helped finance, recruit, transport, and train militant Muslims around the world to fight to bring all Muslims under the rule of Islamic states modeled after the Taliban regime.

Bin Laden also began protesting the continued presence of some twenty thousand American forces stationed in Saudi Arabia where two of the holiest sites of Islam are found in the cities of Mecca and Medina. Bin Laden claimed the United States defaced his holy homeland and accused the Saudi government of complicity with the West at the expense of the Islamic world. The government responded by stripping him of his citizenship and forcing his family to disown him. In 1992 bin Laden left Saudi Arabia for the Sudan to take part in the Islamic revolution underway there under the leadership of Sudanese leader Hassan Turabi.

In the Sudan, he established contact with terrorist groups in other Islamic countries, and al-Qaeda's focus began changing. Now bin Laden became interested in terrorism as a means to pressure the United States to pull back its forces from the region. He also bought several large tracts of farmland and established al-Qaeda training camps. In these training camps, "soldiers" learned about communications and use of arms and explosives and went out into the world to apply their skills. Bin Laden funded their activities against their own governments and against the United States.

The Taliban granted refuge to Osama bin Laden during the mid-1990s. While in Afghanistan, he established al-Qaeda training camps and masterminded worldwide acts of terrorism.

While in the Sudan, al-Qaeda was implicated by the Central Intelligence Agency (CIA) and the Federal Bureau of Investigation (FBI) in the shooting down of two American helicopters in Somalia in 1992, the bombing of the World Trade Center in 1993, and the bombing of the American military installations in Riyadh and Dhahran, Saudi Arabia, in 1995 and 1996. All of these incidents involved loss of American lives.

The United States and Saudi Arabia pressured the Sudanese government to expel bin Laden in order to reduce his power. He moved back to Afghanistan with his family and two hundred of his followers in 1996, where he came under the protection of the Taliban. In exchange for safe haven, bin Laden funded the Taliban and helped their movement grow.

While in Afghanistan, more acts of terrorism were linked to bin Laden's group: the bombing of American embassies in Kenya and Tanzania in 1998 and the attack on the U.S. Navy destroyer USS *Cole* in 2000. The United States retaliated for the embassy bombing by firing seventy cruise missiles against bin Laden's headquarters and training camps in Afghanistan, but failed to kill him.

The War on Terror Begins

Emboldened by success and unafraid to die for their cause, al-Qaeda members continued to carry out bin Laden's terrorist plots. On September 11, 2001, when two hijacked jetliners hit the World Trade Center in New York, another one crashed into the Pentagon, and a fourth one crashed into a field in Pennsylvania, the United States quickly identified bin Laden as the mastermind behind the attack. Knowing that the Taliban hosted bin Laden, the United States demanded that he be surrendered immediately. The Taliban refused, stating that bin Laden was the guest of the Afghan government and he could only leave the country voluntarily. A U.S.-led coalition promptly attacked Afghanistan on October 7, 2001, in Operation Enduring Freedom. Their military objectives were to destroy terrorist training camps and infrastructure, capture al-Qaeda leaders, and oust the Taliban from power.

Operation Enduring Freedom combined airpower, special operations forces, and the anti-Taliban Northern Alliance militia to

Captured Taliban soldiers look out from their jail during Operation Enduring Freedom. The U.S.-led coalition toppled the Taliban in 2001.

achieve these objectives. During the first several days of operation the United States bombed the Taliban's air defense centers, airfields, communication centers, and large concentrations of Taliban/al-Qaeda troops and equipment. After nearly two weeks of fierce air strikes, the U.S. special operations forces entered Afghanistan and established ties with the Northern Alliance militia. They captured Afghanistan's major cities, and on November 21, 2001, the Taliban lost Kabul and surrendered their power. The whereabouts of Osama bin Laden, however, were unknown at the end of the war.

In the streets of Kabul Afghans celebrated the arrival of the U.S. special operations forces and the Northern Alliance militia, who triumphantly entered the capital and secured the city. The Afghans were euphorically optimistic that their years of terror were over and the world would no longer tolerate their suffering.

Although the Northern Alliance and the U.S. special operations forces eventually ousted the Taliban, the aftermath of these

Hamid Karzai

Hamid Karzai was born in Kandahar in 1957. He grew up in Kabul where his father served as a member of the parliament. After the Soviets invaded Afghanistan, he went to India and received undergraduate and graduate degrees in political science. While most of his siblings went to the United States, he settled in Quetta, a Pakistani city close to the border of Afghanistan.

Following the defeat of the Soviets, Karzai was appointed Afghanistan deputy foreign minister in 1992. When the Taliban promised order and stability, Karzai initially supported the Taliban movement. When they began to resort to extreme measures and used violence against Afghans, however, Karzai rallied international support against them.

In the wake of the September 11, 2001, suicide attacks in New York and Washington, Karzai slipped across the border from Quetta, Pakistan, into Afghanistan to get the support of tribal leaders against the Taliban. After the Northern Alliance and the U.S. special operations forces deposed the Taliban regime in November 2001, the representatives of different Afghan groups met in Bonn, Germany, and in December 2001 selected Karzai to be chairman of the Afghan Interim Authority for the next six months. They thought he would be able to rally the support of disparate Afghan groups behind his administration. He also speaks fluent English. He was elected by the members of the *Loya Jirga* as chairman of the Afghan Transition Authority in June 2002.

events leaves Afghanistan at yet another crossroad. Afghan interim president Hamid Karzai has a challenging road ahead of him. Once again, fiercely independent and xenophobic Afghans are facing the presence of foreign troops, the International Security Assistance Force, and U.S. special operations forces in their country. Time will tell whether Afghans will accommodate and welcome their presence or if they will be deemed as yet another set of occupiers who have ravaged their country.

A Diverse Nation

4

Although Afghanistan became independent in 1919, it has yet to achieve political, social, and financial stability. In part, this is due to its unique experience as a colonial buffer state during the nineteenth century and its role as a pawn between the United States and the former Soviet Union during the Cold War. However, another set of factors has also impeded Afghanistan's development and modernization: its geography and cultural diversity. It is a nation of groups with disparate ethnic, linguistic, religious, and tribal traditions.

A major characteristic of Afghan history has been the conflict among these groups. In most cases, loyalty and allegiance to one's group has had precedence over loyalty to the central government, making national unity very difficult to achieve. Perhaps more than any other factor, geophysical, social, and cultural pluralism has caused social and political disagreement, fragmentation of power, and opposition to centralized rule in Afghanistan.

Geography

Afghanistan is a landlocked and mountainous country. The nearest seaport is Karachi, Pakistan, almost seven hundred miles away. The country is bound on the north by Turkmenistan, Uzbekistan, and Tajikistan; on the east by China, Jammu and Kashmir, and Pakistan; on the south by Pakistan; and on the west by Iran.

Tall and forbidding mountains with high plateaus cover about two-thirds of the country. The Hindu Kush range, considered the heart of Afghanistan, bisects the country from northeast to southwest. The Hindu Kush is the westernmost extension of the Karakorum Range in the Himalayas. The Pamirs mountain region, known as the roof of the world because of the many mountain ranges that converge near it, lies at the intersection of four countries—Afghanistan, Pakistan, China, and Tajikistan. The

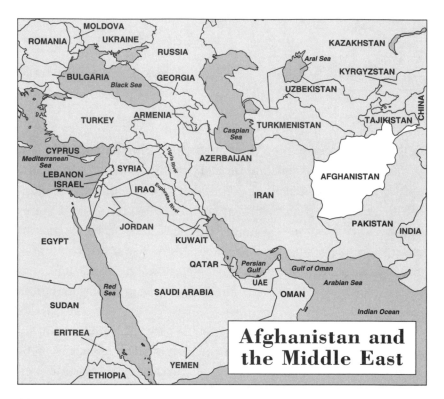

Afghanistan and the Middle East

highest peaks of the Hindu Kush in Afghanistan are over 21,000 feet above sea level and are found in the eastern part of the country. In the middle of the Hindu Kush range, near Kabul, they extend from 13,500 to 18,000 feet above sea level. The average altitude of the Hindu Kush is about 13,500 feet.

Afghanistan's inhospitable geography, landlocked and mountainous, presents obstacles in the way of integration and economic development of the country. This rugged landscape forces most Afghans to live in isolated communities with limited interaction and involvement with surrounding communities and the outside world. In these isolated and mountainous regions, a plethora of different communities with distinct characteristics has developed.

Ethnic Differences

There has never been an accurate count of the population in Afghanistan, but the most common estimate is approximately 26 million as of 2002. These 26 million people exist in a patchwork of over thirty different ethnic groups. Each group has its own language, customs, and tradition. Such incredible disparity has been the source of nearly insurmountable conflict. The main Afghan ethnic groups are Pashtun, Tajik, Hazara, Baluchi, Nuristani, and the Turkic ethnic groups of Uzbek and Turkmens.

These groups are not necessarily contained within Afghanistan: the Pashtuns, for example, are found in both Pakistan and Afghanistan. Some Afghan Tajiks, Uzbeks, and Turkmens live across the border in the former Soviet Union. The Baluchi population is divided among Afghanistan, Iran, and Pakistan. This international distribution of ethnicity has also contributed to the fragmentation of Afghanistan, as surrounding countries get drawn into Afghan national conflicts on behalf of their ethnic groups within the country.

The Pashtuns

The single largest ethnic group is Pashtun, who account for approximately 38 percent of the population. They are concentrated in the southeastern and eastern provinces of Afghanistan but are also scattered in other parts of the country. They speak Pashto, which is an Indo-European language and one of the two official languages of Afghanistan. The other principal language of Afghanistan is Dari (Afghan Persian). The Constitution of 1964 named both Dari and Pashto as official languages.

The southeastern Pashtun tribal groups established the Afghan state in 1747. With the exception of nine months in 1919 and during the civil war (1992–1996) the Pashtuns have maintained their dominance in Afghan politics for several hundred years. Professor Leon B. Poullada observes, "As might be expected, the principle levers of power rest firmly in the hands of Pashtoons. They constitute a preponderant portion of the elite, i.e., the royal family, top government officials, wealthiest merchants and landowners, and most influential chiefs and religious leaders."[23]

Pashtuns and to some extent Hazaras are the only ethnic groups in Afghanistan who are organized by tribes. A tribe is a social organization of people who share a common ancestry, language, culture, and name. Pashtuns are split into three major tribal groups: the Durrani tribe, whose members live primarily in the south; the

Ghilzai tribe found mainly in the eastern part of the country, between Kandahar and Ghazni provinces; and the so-called eastern hill Pashtuns, including the Waziris, Mohmands, Afridis, Khattaks, and Shinwaris.

In the past these tribes have distrusted each other and been involved in power struggles with each other. Outside powers have taken advantage of these differences and supported one tribe over another. Hence, intra-tribal conflict and animosity are contributing factors to the fragmentation of the country, where tribal loyalty has precedence over national loyalty.

Tajiks

Tajiks, who constitute approximately 25 percent of the population, are the second largest ethnic group in Afghanistan. They are widespread in northern, northeastern, and western Afghanistan, and in the valleys north of Kabul. They speak Dari, an Indo-European language. Dari literary means "language of the court."

Tajiks have served as administrators in Afghan governments, but they have been traditionally shut out of the military as well as from high-ranking leadership positions in government. They have only twice produced leaders, once in 1929 and again in 1992. In January 1929 Habibullah Kalakani, known as the "Son of Water-carrier," assumed the throne in Kabul for only nine months. A Pashtun ruler, Muhammad Nadir Shah, soon replaced him. Burhanuddin Rabbani, a Tajik from the northeast, ruled Afghanistan from 1992 to 1996 and was then ousted from the throne by the Taliban.

Hazaras

Hazaras occupy the mountainous central part of the country, known as Hazarajat. They mainly live in the provinces of Bamian, Uruzgan, and Ghazni and are the only major ethnic group entirely contained within Afghanistan. The Hazaras most likely originated from the Mongols, who were a nomadic people unified by Genghis Khan into a powerful nation in the early thirteenth century.

Some historians argue that the armies of Chagatai, Genghis Khan's son, moved across the high central mountains of Afghanistan on their way to conquer India in the later part of the thirteenth

Origin of Dari

Dari language is a member of the Iranian branch of the Indo-European family of languages. It is predominantly spoken in Afghanistan and is one of the two official languages of the country. It is a primary language of Tajiks and Hazaras. It also serves as the means of communication between speakers of the different languages in Afghanistan.

Dari is related to Farsi, the language of Iran. In the past, Dari was a spoken language while Farsi was the written and scholarly language. With the advent of Islam in the seventh century, Arabic replaced Farsi for many years as the dominant language in the region, but Dari is still common.

century. Some of these soldiers stayed in the area and created the modern Hazara people, who make up about 10 to 15 percent of the population of the country. They speak a Dari dialect with Turkic and Mongol additions, called Hazaragi.

Hazaras are also the largest Shia community in Afghanistan. Shias are the minority sect of Islam, and Hazaras have a long history of political and religious persecution within Afghanistan. According to anthropology professor Grant Farr, "The Hazara situation in Afghanistan can be characterized as a pariah status, underprivileged socially, economically, and culturally. They occupy the lowest status in Afghan society and suffer considerable discrimination and prejudice."[24] In the past, Hazaras were often used as slaves and servants. In their mountainous homeland, they are sheep breeders, but many of them have migrated to the cities, where they perform menial jobs.

Other Ethnic Groups

Other ethnic groups include Turkic, Baluchi, and Nuristani. The two major Turkic ethnic groups, descending from Turkey, are the Uzbeks and the Turkmens. They constitute approximately 10 percent of the Afghan population. The most populous of the Turkic groups in Afghanistan is the Uzbeks. Many migrated into Afghanistan under pressure from czarist Russia and the Soviet Union in the early part of the twentieth century. They inhabit the

Nuristanis inhabit remote areas in northeastern Afghanistan. Their light skin and blue eyes may be attributed to interaction with Greeks during Alexander the Great's reign.

northern provinces of Afghanistan, including Balkh, Shabirghan, and Maimana. They speak different Turkic dialects, closely related to the language spoken in Turkey. The Uzbeks are primarily farmers and noted breeders of horses and karakul sheep. The Turkmens, who emigrated from the Soviet Union in the 1920s, are also karakul breeders and skilled carpet weavers. They have produced Afghanistan's most valued traditional exports, karakul pelts and handwoven carpets.

Baluchis inhabit the desert areas of the southwest and they are divided among Afghanistan, Pakistan, and Iran. They are famous for camel breeding and for their handwoven carpets. They speak Baluchi, a language belonging to the Iranian group of the Indo-Iranian family of languages.

Finally, the Nuristanis inhabit relatively isolated villages in deep, narrow mountain valleys in northeastern Afghanistan, neighboring Chitral, Pakistan. They have a separate language and different culture. They speak Dardic dialects belonging to a distinct branch of the Indo-Iranian language family. They kept their polytheistic (worship of many gods) religion until 1896, when King Abd ar-Rahman Khan forced them to convert to Islam and renamed their region Nuristan (Land of Light) from Kafiristan (Land of Pagans).

Alexander the Great invited the young men of Nuristan to join his army while in Afghanistan on his way to invade India. The young Nuristanis proved their fighting ability with distinction. Many Greek customs as well as the light skin, blue eyes, and blond or red hair found among the Nuristanis today may date from this encounter with the Greeks in the time of Alexander the Great.

The plethora of Afghan ethnic groups has hindered the emergence of a homogenous, integrated society. Instead, loyalty to one's group replaces loyalty to the nation. As a result, the Afghan governments have failed to develop a strong, centralized, and unified nation-state, and the country has remained in transition for most of its modern existence.

Religious Diversity

The population of Afghanistan is fragmented not only into different ethnic groups but also into different religious groups. Afghanistan is a predominantly Muslim country, with approximately 85 percent of the population Sunni Muslim and the remainder Jafari "Twelver" Shia or Ismaili "Sevener" Shia Muslim. In addition, there are small groups of Hindus and Sikhs (originally traders from India) in Afghanistan. These different religious groups often clash with each other over the sharing and distribution of power and the composition of government. These schisms further contribute to the chaos in Afghanistan.

Islam started expanding in the seventh century under the leadership of Ali, the second caliph of Islam and successor to the prophet Muhammad. It was not until the ninth century that the ideas of Islam effectively reached Kabul, the present capital of Afghanistan. By the tenth century, the Afghan population had become largely Muslim. Today, Afghan Muslims belong to one of the two major sects of Islam: the Sunni (the orthodox or traditionalists) and the Shia (the heterodox or the partisans of Caliph Ali).

Sunni

Sunnis make up the majority of Muslims around the world. The root of the word is *sunna*, meaning "custom." Sunni Muslims believe in the five pillars of Islam, the framework of Muslim life. The first pillar is faith. Muslims believe that there is no god worthy of worship except Allah (the Arabic word for God). Prayer constitutes the second pillar of Islam. Prayers are performed five times a day and are a direct link between the worshiper and Allah. When praying, Muslims are required to face in the direction of Mecca, a city in Saudi Arabia where the Kaaba or the "House of Allah" is located. Another pillar is almsgiving. This involves the payment each year of 2.5 percent of one's wealth to charity. The fourth pillar of Islam is fasting. Every year in the month of Ramadan, Muslims fast from dawn to dusk, abstaining from food, drink, and sexual relations. Ramadan is also a sacred month because it commemorates the time when Allah first revealed the Koran, the Muslim holy book, to the prophet Muhammad. The last pillar is pilgrimage to Mecca. It is an obligation only for Muslims who are physically and financially able to perform it.

Shia

Although the Shias adhere to many of the same practices as the Sunnis, they believe in a different clergy system. The Shias split from the Sunnis not long after the death of the prophet Muhammad in 632. When determining who should lead the new community of Muslims in the wake of the prophet's death, the Sunnis supported any righteous and wise Muslim as a successor. Others, however, supported Ali, the Prophet's cousin and son-in-law (*Shia* literally refers to "partisans of Ali"). The Shias argued that leadership after the prophet Muhammad should be entrusted to a member of the prophet's family and that only a descendant of the prophet has the right to rule.

This partisanship caused a rift that has since divided the two groups of Muslims. Although leadership succession was the basis of Shia/Sunni differences, further variations in Islamic doctrine, legal traditions, ritual, and practice have developed over the centuries.

Jafari Shiites are the dominant Shia group in Afghanistan. They make up 15 percent of the population and are concentrated in central and western Afghanistan. In the past the minority religious groups, such as the Shia Hazaras, have been persecuted in Afghanistan. The ruling Pashtuns, a Sunni ethnic group, forbade Shia religious practices and made it impossible for Shia groups to pursue careers in the armed forces or politics.

Most recently, after the Taliban captured Herat and the Hazarajat, many Shias were massacred and others forcibly resettled in the Sunni-majority areas of neighboring provinces. Professor Grant Farr observes, "In January of 2001 the Taliban entered the Yakaolang district of the Hazarajat. [They] detained 300 civilians, . . . and then shot them by firing squad in public view."[25] The Shia groups have thus traditionally distrusted and refused to cooperate with the central government to strengthen its power.

Tribalism

Another factor that contributes to the lack of a strong central government is tribalism. Although all Afghans do not consider them tribal members, most Pashtuns are tribalized. Because the Pashtuns have historically dominated government, other nontribalized ethnic groups have had to learn the nuances of tribalism in order to deal with them.

The tribe is organized in a pyramidal structure based on common genealogy. Descent is claimed from the father's side of the family. A Pashtun is first related to his extended family, then to his clan, and then to his tribe. A person marries and forms bonds within this clan. The power of the tribe is exceptionally strong because tribal loyalty is an important source of its strength and cohesiveness.

Different clans within a tribe choose an elder or chief, the *malik*. The *maliks* in turn elect a khan, who is the leader of the tribe. They act as representatives, conveying tribal demands and wishes to the government. The khan keeps contact with the officials in the provincial capital or the capital city, Kabul. Tribal problems and issues are worked out through the institution of *Jirga* or council.

Tribalism is the most important traditional institution in Afghanistan. Tribes provide a sense of solidarity, security, and political power to their members. At the same time, tribalism has prevented the emergence of national awareness and a unified state of mind. For most Afghans, especially Pashtuns, tribal identity and loyalty precede national identity and national consciousness.

Pashtunwali

Tribalism also involves tribal ideology, customs, and common law. All these elements of Pashtun tribalism are included in *Pashtunwali,* or Pashtun tribal code. *Pashtunwali* sets the limits of acceptable behavior within the community and governs the relations between tribes. The main components of *Pashtunwali* are *Jirga, badal, melmastia, nanawati,* and *nang.*

The *Jirga* is a form of local government, a kind of judicial and parliamentary body. It makes decisions in all disputes, including disputes over women, murder, and ownership of land. Professor Leon B. Poullada notes, "The composition of the jirga may vary for different purposes. In general it must have representatives from all families who are involved or may be affected by the decision. In major matters such as war and peace, major segments of the tribe must be represented. Decisions are not taken by 'vote' but rather by consensus." [26]

Afghan governments have nationalized these *Jirgas* to deal with extraordinary and emergency situations. When they are convened at the national level, they are called *Loya Jirga* or grand council. This tribal institution is viewed by government as the best available cross section of the ethnically diverse population to deliberate and decide on issues of overriding national importance. Moreover, Afghan governments have used *Loya Jirgas* to get approval and rally the support of Afghans behind government-initiated policies. For instance, it has been convened in the past to discuss and approve social reforms, new government, or a constitution. In other words, Afghan governments have used this tribal institution as a way of persuasion in order to gain legitimacy.

There is an Afghan proverb that says, "An Afghan took his revenge after one hundred years, he was still saying he rushed it."

This proverb refers to the *Pashtunwali* code of *badal,* which is translated as "revenge." This tribal code gives everyone the right to balance justice. It is based on the principle of "an eye for an eye, a tooth for a tooth." Even minor infractions warrant revenge, as they have insulted someone's honor, a grave crime in *Pashtunwali.*

The obligation to take revenge never ceases and knows no limitation of time or space until restitution is obtained. Researcher

THE FIRST *LOYA JIRGA*

The first and most famous *Loya Jirga* took place in 1747, when Pashtun tribal members and leaders gathered in the southern city of Kandahar to select a king for Afghanistan. After nine days of debates over who should be chosen, the tribal chiefs chose the only man to remain silent throughout the entire debate, Ahmed Shah Durrani, the man who founded the state of Afghanistan. His selection established the political domination of the Pashtun, an ethnic group that remain among the ruling elite of Afghanistan. The last *Loya Jirga* was convened in Kabul in June 2002. It lasted for a week. It consisted of sixteen hundred delegates, most of them elected, who came together to select a new temporary president and to confirm the president's cabinet.

Loya Jirga *representatives vote during an election in Kabul.*

Ahmed Shah Massoud, the most famous mujhid, resisted the Soviet occupation and commanded Northern Alliance forces against the Taliban. He was assassinated in 2001.

Sultan A. Aziz observes, "This concept is enforced regardless of time, space, and cost."[27] Failure to take the prescribed measure of revenge brings *sharm,* or dishonor, to all upon whom this obligation lies.

Another important part of the traditional code of Pashtun behavior is *melmastia,* or hospitality. Based on this code of conduct, a traveler must be received and cared for. His host must protect him from his enemies even at the cost of the host's life. Otherwise the requirement of *melmastia* will not have been met. Anyone that is a guest in one's house and country, and comes peacefully, is provided with whatever the host has in his possession in terms of food and shelter. When the Taliban refused to turn over Osama bin Laden to the United States in 2001, they were abiding by the code of *melmastia.*

The fourth aspect of the *Pashtunwali* is called *nanawati,* or asylum. It is the tribal practice to end revenge when revenge is carried too far. It must be given to the deadliest enemy who has voluntarily placed himself in one's power and requested a safe haven. It is also a form of asking for forgiveness. If an individual has committed a heinous crime and comes to the home of the victim accompanied by elders, the victim must forgive the defendant.

The last code of *Pashtunwali* is called *nang.* It stands for honor, bravery, and valor. It is one's self-esteem. All offenses committed against one's honor will be severely dealt with. *Nang* also means honor and protection of women. According to the tribal code, a woman is an extension of a man's honor and must be protected at whatever cost. For example, when the government started to advocate women's liberation during the 1920s and the 1950s, Pashtuns were offended and rebelled against the government.

The presence of the tribal code of behavior prevents a standardized code of behavior, established by the government, to take root in the country. As a result, *Pashtunwali* contributes to the large problem of Afghan disunity. It provides and encourages a sense of loyalty and cohesiveness to one's tribal code of behavior and values at the expense of a national standard of conduct.

Society of Warlords

Another impact of ethnicity and tribalism on national unity is the emergence of warlords in Afghanistan. Warlordism, a political phenomenon that developed during the civil war, contributes to further anarchy and disintegration of Afghan society. After the armed mujahideen captured Kabul in 1992, they turned their guns against each other, vying for power. These clashes between armed groups were organized along ethno-religious cleavages, that is, Pashtun versus Tajik and Sunni versus Shia. The commanders of different factions of mujahideen carved out chunks of Afghanistan for themselves. In these, they established their own fiefdoms (a term that refers to lands given to lords by the king during the period of feudalism in Europe) with military and financial assistance they acquired from neighboring states.

Each warlord recruits his militia largely from his own ethnic group and rules his territory, which is usually populated by his ethnic group. The warlords are accepted by their constituents because they share a common kinship, ethnicity, and religion. Each warlord governs the day-to-day activity of his territory by dispensing justice and providing safety, security, and essential services. The most famous warlord is Ahmed Shah Massoud. He was an ethnic Tajik who fought bravely with his militia against the Soviet Union during its occupation of Afghanistan. He also commanded the Northern Alliance forces against the Taliban from his

Hamid Karzai rallied international support against the Taliban. He was elected interim president of Afghanistan in June 2002.

base in the northeast until he was assassinated on September 9, 2001. Abdul Rashid Dostum was the warlord of Uzbeks in northern Afghanistan. Unlike other warlords, he fought with Soviets during the Soviet occupation of Afghanistan. Another warlord was Ismail Khan, a Shia Tajik warlord. He led an uprising against the Soviet occupation in Herat. Last but not least, Gulbuddin Hekmatyar, an ethnic Pashtun, was the leader of the Islamic Party and the most notorious of the warlords. After the defeat of the last Communist government, Hekmatyar fought against the government of mujahideen and helped reduce Kabul to rubble. He has since gone into hiding in Iran. The Federal Bureau of Investigation (FBI) is presently looking for him and recently placed his name on the list of the most-wanted international terrorists.

Like tribalism and *Pashtunwali,* the institution of warlords contributes to disunity among Afghans. The warlords constantly wage war against each other for expansion of their territories and ultimate control of the central government. Therefore, warlords are a major obstacle to developing a national system of leadership and integration of the country.

Grasping for Unity

Following the United States' successful military campaign against the Taliban in October 2001, power returned to the warlords, each in control of a specific region of the country. Although there is the Afghan Transition Authority, headed by Hamid Karzai, it has been unable to expand its authority beyond the capital city of Kabul. As a result, Dostum continues to control most of five northern provinces; Ismail Khan and his allies rule another five western and northwestern provinces; and the remaining warlords and their militias are in control of other regions of Afghanistan. This political situation makes it difficult to create a strong central government to lead Afghanistan into unification, political and economic development, and modernization.

Geography, ethnicity, religious diversity, tribalism, and emergence of warlordism have shaped present-day Afghanistan with far-reaching effects on Afghan society. While these factors provide a sense of solidarity, security, and political power to their respective community members, they prevent the emergence of national consciousness and unified state of mind. For most Afghans, identity and loyalty to one's ethnicity, religion, and tribe take precedence over national identity and national awareness, which means Afghanistan will most likely experience continued political and economic fragmentation.

Women in Afghanistan 5

Conservative social customs and traditions do not allow Afghan women to fully participate in social, economic, cultural, and political life. Regardless of what Afghan law may permit women to do, tradition dictates that they stay within the confines of their homes and limit their activities to raising children and tending to their household duties. According to custom, only a man can be head of a family and make decisions for family members.

Researcher Huma Ahmed Ghosh states that, "Tribal laws viewed marriages as alliances between groups; women were pawned into marriages, not allowed to divorce, total obedience to the husband and his family was expected, and they were prevented from getting any education. Women were perceived as the receptacles of 'honor', hence they stayed in the domestic sphere, observed the veil and were voiceless."[28]

Past Afghan governments, however, attempted to introduce various reforms in order to improve the position of women in the society. For example, the Constitution of 1964 guaranteed that all Afghans, without discrimination and privilege, have equal rights and obligations before the law. With the emergence of the Taliban, however, women who had asserted their rights and entered public life were forced back into veils and seclusion. The post-Taliban government of Hamid Karzai has attempted to restore the rights of Afghan women, but there is a lot of work to be done before the society, including many of the women themselves, is ready to accept such changes.

Traditional Lifestyle of Afghan Women

Traditional Afghan society is patriarchal (rule of family by men). In traditional Afghan families girls are less valuable than boys. A boy will pass his name on to his children, thereby giving an heir to the family's property. He is also his parents' future social security, in that he will help and take care of them when they grow old. A girl, however, does not have this value, and thus a mother does not feel secure in her husband's family by delivering a daughter. According to an Afghan proverb, "A girl belongs to the people"; that is, she will be married off at a young age and move from her parents' home to live with her husband and in-laws.

In traditional Afghan families, unmarried girls stay home and help their mothers perform house chores. According to researcher Fahima Vorgetts, "From the age of five or six, I was initiated into the responsibilities of cooking and taking care of younger siblings. So were my female cousins, sisters, and friends. But my brothers and male cousins had no such responsibilities."[29] Some families, especially those who live in Kabul, allow their daughters to have limited education. Once they become teenagers, though, they are pulled out of schools by their parents and stay at home until they are married.

Women and Honor

Most Afghans believe that the honor of a family resides in the conduct of its women. Honor depends on a woman remaining chaste. If she is violated in any way, the men of the family risk being considered weak. This is because the honor of a man is based on how well he protects the women in his care. Premarital affairs will be perceived as an insult not only to family pride but also to the entire clan and tribe. According to researcher Erika Knabe, "Many of the feuds between [Pashtun] groups are instigated by a violation of the [nang] related to women. These feuds are more critical than quarrels over land and water. In cases where the female is suspected of complicity in the affair, she is punished severely or even killed."[30]

In order to protect one's honor, for example, it is considered inappropriate for a male to mention the names of female members of a family when speaking to strangers. Researcher Jan Goodwin remarks that "Disturbing was the fury I caused when I approached a young male acquaintance while he was with friends to inquire after his sister's health when she had been sick. He refused to acknowledge me, and next time I saw him, he stormed at me that I had dared mention his sister, even used her name, in front of other men. He insisted my behavior had shamed him."[31]

Marriage and Divorce

Most marriages are arranged between families. Traditionally, parents make the final decision regarding which households their children marry into. Scholar Barnett R. Rubin observes that "In one sample of educated women in Kabul in the early 1970s, only 24 percent had any say in their choice of husbands."[32] When arranging a marriage, most families prefer that the bride and groom are from the same ethnic group, religious sect, and social class. Women are also frequently married to relatives. The preferred would-be husband is the paternal first cousin, because the boy and the girl know each other very well.

Arranged marriages are not an Islamic requirement. There is not a verse in the Koran that calls for this practice. A Muslim woman also cannot be forced into a marriage. These are cultural and traditional phenomenon that exist in Afghanistan and many other Muslim and non-Muslim countries.

Once female relatives of a would-be groom establish contact with a girl and her family and are favorably impressed with her, the men of both families get involved in negotiations. They decide upon the engagement and marriage dates; the *toyana,* or bride-price; and *mahr,* or dowry. *Mahr* is a kind of social insurance. It is an amount of money to be paid to the bride in the event of a divorce. It is also set aside for her as an expression of a man's sense of responsibility, obligation, and serious desire to marry her. The *mahr*—which can consist of cash, land, houses, gardens, and the like—is determined in the marriage contract, the *nekah nama.*

A traditional Afghan bride does not meet her groom until the end of the wedding ceremony when she first sees him in a mirror, held under her veil, as the couple is declared man and wife. Even if she is engaged to a paternal first cousin, once the engagement is made formal, the couple will not see each other until the wedding night. They consummate their marriage on the night of their wedding. The bride must be a virgin and she must prove it publicly. According to researcher Jan Goodwin, "A white sheet daubed with her blood from the breaking of her hymen is passed among relatives the day after the wedding [to prove in public that she is a virgin]."[33] If there is any doubt about her chastity, the husband can send her back to her parents' home, and divorce will follow.

A married woman usually lives with her in-laws until her husband can afford his own house. (A man is required to financially support his wife). While living with her in-laws she must please her husband and his relatives so that she is well liked by them. Jan Goodwin observes that, "Once she is married, an Afghan woman will see her own family again only with the permission of her husband, which he may or may not grant."[34]

Divorce is not very common in Afghanistan, as it is considered shameful. A man has the right to divorce. He does not have to provide any reason to the court. When a man initiates divorce, people often think that something must have been wrong with the woman; otherwise the husband would not have divorced her. A woman also has the right to seek divorce, but it rarely occurs, as few women are financially able to support themselves after the divorce.

A groom is led on horseback to his wedding ceremony. In traditional Afghan society, all marriages are arranged.

The Place of Women in Society

Afghan tradition and Islam require women to stay in purdah, or seclusion. Purdah is a Persian word and can have a wide range of interpretations. The seclusion required by purdah can be achieved by wearing a modest veil over one's hair, or it can describe the system whereby women are not allowed to leave their homes except in emergency situations. As part of the Afghan tradition of purdah, Afghan women wear the chador as a garment that covers the body from head to toe with only a textile net in front of the eyes.

Both Afghan cultural traditions and Islam consider purdah a matter of honor, dignity, purity, and chastity. According to Islam, a woman should stir only her husband's passions. She should not expose her physical attractions before strangers. According to the Koran (24:30–31), "And say to the believing women, that they cast down their eyes and guard their private parts, and reveal not their adornment save such as is outward; and let them cast their veils over their bosoms, and not reveal their adornment save to

The Chador

The word "chador" comes from the Persian word, *chadar,* meaning scarf. The garment is usually made out of silk or cotton.

Before the Taliban's decree required all women to wear it, the chador was an urban garment worn by most women who lived in the cities. These women wore the chador as a sign of status and sophistication. Women in rural areas of Afghanistan wore a variation of the chador, made up of a large rectangle of material, which is dropped over the head, hair, and the upper part of a woman's body. It can be pulled over the face if modesty demands such action.

The chador started to disappear from Kabul in 1959, especially among the educated women who preferred to wear Western clothing. These women donned head scarves, dark sunglasses, coats, gloves, and stockings. In the 1970s, scarves and sunglasses were left at home and miniskirts became fashionable on the streets of Kabul and on the Kabul University campus. This trend continued until Afghanistan became engulfed in the long civil war and the Taliban movement emerged.

their husbands, or their fathers, or their husbands' fathers." This Koranic verse has been interpreted differently among Islamic states and thus has many variations in practice.

Seclusion of women has a wide range of social, economic, and political implications. There is limited interaction and commingling between the sexes. Women very often interact only with other women. Women are not allowed to venture outside, especially in rural areas of the country, without being escorted by a male relative. Women are prevented from becoming active members of society, as they cannot attend school, hold jobs, hold political office, or participate in nearly any other aspect of life outside of their homes. Researcher Erika Knabe observes, "In many areas of Afghansitan particularly in rural towns, the confinement of women is almost absolute. Men do the necessary family shopping for food and clothing. A husband may even forbid his wife to pay an occasional visit to her parents."[35]

Government as an Agent of Change

Past Afghan governments have attempted to take specific actions to improve the conditions of women in the country. Amanullah Khan and his wife, Soraya, were the first Afghan king and queen who seriously attempted to change the lifestyle of Afghan women. Amanullah Khan declared that women might choose not to be seen in public wearing a chador. His own wife, Queen Soraya, appeared unveiled and commingled with men on a trip to Europe.

Both the king and the queen advocated schools for girls and work outside the home. The first school for girls, Malalai, was opened in 1921 in Kabul. By 1927 there were two new primary schools for girls with several hundred enrolled. The school operated under the guidance of Queen Soraya, who also founded the first women's weekly magazine called *Irshad-i-Niswan,* or the *Guide for Women,* in 1921.

King Amanullah also established the first women's society called *Anjuman-i-Himayah-i-Niswan* or Female Defense Association. The association was placed under the direct supervision of the queen. According to scholar Senzil Nawid, "The immediate purpose of the [association] was to give women self-respect, competence and assertiveness; the long-term objective was to prepare them for future political activities." [36]

In a speech before a group of Afghan women during the country's independence celebrations, Queen Soraya spoke about the role of women in national development. She stated, "Do not think ... that our nation needs only men to serve it. Women should also take part as women did in the early years of Islam. The valuable services rendered by women are recounted throughout history from which we learn that we were not created solely for pleasure and comfort. From their examples we learn that we must all contribute toward the development of our nation and that this cannot be done without being equipped with knowledge." [37]

To further these goals, the King established the marriage law of 1921, which abolished the tradition common among the tribes by which a widow was forced to marry a close relative. Another provision of the new marriage law prohibited polygamy if injustice between wives was an issue. The would-be husband was required to present two witnesses in the court to testify to the fact that he would treat both the present and future wives equally. Only after the court's approval was he allowed to marry an additional wife.

In 1928 the king and queen's sustained attempt at reforms, however, triggered a rebellion from the religious and traditional leaders. All girls' schools were closed. The king was eventually toppled and forced to leave Afghanistan. Thus, for the next thirty years the king and queen's reforms affecting Afghan women were abandoned.

The Unveiling of Women
Afghan women continued to wear the chador and remain in seclusion until 1959, when Prime Minister Muhammad Daud Khan launched a revolution for Afghan women by announcing his support for the voluntary removal of the chador and an end to the practice of purdah. Daud Khan was determined to modernize Afghan society, and the liberation of Afghan women was part of his modernization plan. On August 24, 1959, on the occasion of Afghanistan's Independence Day in Kabul, Daud Khan, other

members of the royal family, the cabinet, and high-ranking army officers appeared in public with their unveiled wives and daughters. Later, hundreds of educated, unveiled women appeared in public in Kabul and in other urban areas of the country. Researcher Parwin Ali Majrooh observes that "Removal of the veil was gradually expanded in a voluntary manner in all girls' schools, the women's faculties of Kabul University, and further in provincial centers and towns. It was accepted by the majority of educated people and became a popular trend within a short period of time."[38] Although schools for girls remained segregated, those students who wished to appear unveiled were allowed to wear a black uniform with a white head scarf.

The Constitution of 1964 and Women

Five years after the unveiling of women in 1959, a new constitution confirmed the new role of women in Afghan society. The Constitution of 1964, drawn up by a constitutional advisory committee under the leadership of King Muhammad Zahir Shah and promulgated by the *Loya Jirga,* stated that all Afghans, without discrimination or preference, have equal rights and obligations before the law. Among other rights, the constitution guaranteed women dignity, compulsory education, freedom to work, and the right to dress as they wished. This provision had dramatic consequences

Polygamy and Islam

During the early period of Islam, the practice of polygamy (the taking of more than one wife at a time) arose as a natural consequence of men losing their lives in tribal wars. Without husbands, many women and children were left behind without any support. Therefore, other men took these women in as their wives and adopted their children.

As such, the practice is permitted in Islam in a restricted form. A prerequisite for polygamy is equality of treatment and provisions for the wives. The Koran states in chapter 4, verse 2, "Marry women of your choice, two, three, or four, but if you fear that you shall not be able to deal justly with them then only one." Because of this precondition to polygamy, it is not widely practiced in Islamic countries.

for Afghan women. A typical unveiled woman might have been seen wearing a raincoat, stylish sunglasses, a fashionable head scarf, and gloves.

After the constitution went into effect, female student enrollment also increased at the University of Kabul. Women could take coeducational classes taught by both male and female professors. In addition, more female students were sent abroad on scholarship to study. The introduction of coeducational classes provided the opportunity for male and female students to commingle. As a result, there were fewer arranged marriages, and more parents left the choice of suitors to their daughters.

Women could also run for office. During the parliamentary elections of the 1960s, several female candidates were elected to the Afghan parliament. Kubra Nurza'ai, became the first female secretary of health in 1966. Urban women took an active part in public life and gained access to positions in the fields of

Afghan women listen to a lecture at a nursing school in Pakistan. Prior to the Taliban, women were able to study in Afghanistan and abroad.

health care, education, and administration. According to scholar Nancy Hatch Dupree, "Over the years increasing numbers of educated women emerged to work in government and business, as secretaries and judges, hair dressers and diplomats, entertainers and parliamentarians. Women were employed in some factories, including ceramics, fruit packaging, pharmaceuticals and housing construction." [39]

The Communist Government and Women's Rights

The Communist government in Afghanistan, which lasted from 1978 to 1992, attempted to further expand the rights of women through a series of directives or decrees. Decree number seven ensured equal rights for women and improved their position in the society. The decree prohibited arranged marriages or marriages of men under eighteen or women under sixteen years of age and said that no one should be forced into marriage. Decree number seven also established legal penalties of imprisonment for violating the decree's provisions.

In order to mobilize Afghan women, the Communist regime also established the Democratic Organization of Afghan Women (DOAW). The organization actively encouraged women to attend political rallies in support of the government's domestic and foreign policies. It also attempted to extend civic and political education to women and to help them understand their rights and responsibilities. One of the active members of the DOAW was Anahita Ratibzad, minister of social affairs in the Communist government and a former member of parliament. She led the effort in rallying the support of women behind the Communist government policies.

These new reforms were an urban phenomenon and faced strong opposition from the less progressive sector of Afghan society. Most Afghans, especially in the countryside, considered the Communist government a godless regime in an Islamic country and an extension of the Soviet empire. Therefore, they fiercely resented these reforms, and they refused to consider the Communist government legitimate. Led by mujahideen, uprisings and rebellion against the Communist government broke out in different parts of the country. In the chaos that ensued, the new rights and freedoms women had achieved quickly deteriorated and were summarily denied by the Taliban when they assumed power in 1996.

Women Under the Taliban

The goal of the Taliban movement was to install a pure Islamic society in Afghanistan based on an ultraconservative interpretation of Islamic law or the *Shari'a*. Once in power, the Taliban began to enforce these harshly repressive laws, especially regarding women.

The Taliban denied women all basic fundamental rights, including the right to work, the right to education, the right to health, the right to travel, and the right to recreation. Researcher Nancy Hatch Dupree states that "The first decrees announced by [the Taliban] required women to curtail their movements in public, and then only when decently covered and in the company of close family relations. As an extension of these restrictions, female work outside the home [was] proscribed and girls' schools [were] closed."[40]

The Taliban enforced strict gender segregation rules. They dismissed women from jobs where they might have to interact with men and confined them to jobs where they would only come in contact with other women. Most women lost their jobs and were reduced to begging on the streets of major cities. Reporter Saira Shah told the BBC in 2001, "The first thing you notice when you come to Kabul is the ghost-like figures in their blue shroud-like burqas [chadors], begging in the streets."[41] Another consequence of unemployment was an increase in the number of suicides by women who were unable to support their children.

Under the Taliban, no woman could see a male doctor. However, there were not enough female doctors in the country to treat all female patients. As a result, many women died of treatable medical conditions because doctors were not available for them.

Afghan women wait outside a health clinic. Because the Taliban prohibited women from seeing male doctors, many died of curable illnesses while awaiting treatment.

There was also a shortage of nurses in male wards in most hospitals because female nurses were not allowed to take care of male patients.

Restrictions Abound

Women were soon shut out of education as well. All girls' schools were closed. Some girls secretly attended home-based schools in Kabul, but at great risk. They could be beaten, imprisoned, or even murdered. When the Taliban found out about the existence of such schools, they closed down most of them. Only girls under the age of twelve were allowed to attend the schools that remained open. However, the curriculum was limited to reading skills so that the girls could read the Koran.

Women were not allowed to travel in private vehicles with male passengers, nor could a male tailor take a woman's measurements or sew women's clothes. The Taliban also closed thirty-two women's public bathhouses. Even the faces of women disappeared from public view. Their pictures could not be printed in newspapers or books or hung on the walls of houses and shops. Once again women had to hide themselves beneath the chador.

The chador consists of three parts sewn together: a skullcap; an embroidered face cover, perforated to permit breathing and limited vision; and a body cover with an embroidered front. Wearing a chador in the heat of Afghan summer can be uncomfortable and cumbersome. One can even be suffocated for lack of adequate oxygen beneath it. In a chador, it is even difficult to move around freely and cross streets or walk up stairs. Bright-colored clothing, makeup, and high-heeled shoes, even under the chador, were prohibited because the Taliban believed them to be sexually stimulating colors and might corrupt a man.

Failure to Comply

The Taliban administered a variety of punishments against those who undermined their prescribed regulations. The religious police either beat or flogged those caught not wearing the chador. Fatima, an Afghan woman who taught English until the Taliban

Under Taliban rule, women disappeared from Afghan society. Forced to conceal themselves with a chador, they were beaten if they were not properly covered.

came to power, observes, "One day, I went to the market with a friend. Our [chadors] revealed more of our faces than what the Taliban police found acceptable. So they beat us with sticks—we only pulled the [chador] up because the heat was stifling." [42] Women who were caught stealing or robbing had their hands amputated as punishment. Many women were stoned to death or shot for alleged adultery. The Taliban carried out these punishments in soccer stadiums in the presence of thousands of spectators—most of whom were forced to attend. The Taliban used public execution to instill fear in people and deter crimes.

The Taliban's treatment of Afghan women was so harsh and repressive that it was condemned by leading human rights organizations, who called the Taliban draconian measures gender apartheid, comparing them to South Africa's apartheid (official policy of racial segregation to promote and maintain white superiority) crimes of the 1980s. To this the Taliban replied that Allah had defined and determined women's rights, not the United States or the United Nations or the European states. Author Ahmed Rashid observes that "[Mullah Mohammed] Omar [the Taliban leader] and his colleagues transposed their own milieu, their own experience, or lack of it, with women, to the entire country and justified their policies through the Koran." [43]

The Taliban's use of repression against women, however, was a result of ignorance and hateful manipulation and not real religious knowledge and commitment. The Taliban took these harsh measures to supposedly restore honor and dignity to women. They claimed that by allowing women to wear makeup and skimpy clothes, the West had made them into objects of man's lust and desires. The Taliban thought the West exploited women by forcing them to work. Consequently, said the Taliban, Western women lose their personalities and sense of identity and family. Addressing the West, the Taliban frequently stated that the West had no right to force upon Afghans their own failed values.

Women After the Taliban

Women existed under these conditions until November 2001, when the Taliban were defeated by the Northern Alliance, backed by U.S.

Since the defeat of the Taliban in 2001, the status of Afghan women has improved. They are able to attend school and seek government employment.

special operations forces. By and large, the status of women in society has improved since the downfall of the Taliban regime. The government of Hamid Karzai has taken steps to restore the rights of Afghan women. They are now able to work for government and nonprofit organizations. Several thousand schools have been opened to both boys and girls. Several universities have opened their doors to both male and female students. Moreover, several women occupy senior positions in government. For the first time in Afghan history, a Ministry for Women's Affairs has been established. The principal goals of the ministry are to lay the groundwork for sustainable employment and promote women's rights.

Karzai has signed the Declaration of the Afghan Women's Rights, a document that states in part that the women of Afghanistan are entitled to equality. They have the right to equal protection under the law, freedom of movement, freedom of speech, and political participation. They also have the right to wear or not wear the chador or a head scarf. By signing this important document, Karzai expressed the commitment of his government to restore the rights and freedom of Afghan women.

Although official moves have been taken to restore the rights of women, it will take longer to change the attitudes of both men and women who have lived and suffered during the past twenty-three years. Some men, especially in rural areas, still resist expanding educational opportunities for women, and several schools for girls have been attacked with rockets or set on fire in different provinces. Male teachers have also received death threats for teaching in girls' schools. Many women are still afraid to venture outside unveiled because they think that the Taliban are still around in the country, or fear reprisal from men who disapprove of the government's new policies.

After more than twenty years of destruction and war, the government has an enormous challenge ahead regarding women's rights. Only time will tell if the post-Taliban government is seriously interested in restoring the civil rights and liberties of women, and if the Afghan people will support them in their endeavor.

Epilogue
Rebuilding for Peace

Today, Afghanistan finds itself at yet another crossroad in its long, unsteady history. Faced with many critical obstacles, it will take serious international commitment to bolster the country with the infrastructure and necessary resources to ensure its success. As important as cooperation and support from other nations is, it is Afghans themselves who must unite as a nation if they hope to achieve peace.

Establishing Security

One of the pressing issues facing the government is security. During the civil war the Afghan armed forces were replaced by private militias which divided and destroyed the country. In order to expand the power of the central government over the entire country and enforce a ban on these private militias, the country needs a national army. Many of the very same warlords, ousted from power by the Taliban, are returning to their old lairs. They have seized control of some provinces and maintain their own militias, sources of income, and autonomous administrations. Conflict between ethnic groups and remnants of the Taliban and al-Qaeda also threaten the government's stability and authority.

The UN Security Council resolution of December 20, 2001, authorized the deployment of the International Security Assistance Force (ISAF) to provide security, but only in Kabul. The ISAF consists of approximately five thousand peacekeeping troops drawn from over twenty European nations and Turkey. Another security force currently present in the country consists of over eight thousand U.S. special operations forces. They initially led the coalition forces that ousted the Taliban from power. Now they are focused on the pursuit of remnants of Taliban and al-Qaeda operatives.

Lakhdar Brahimi, the UN envoy to Afghanistan, warns that security issues are threatening the Afghan peace process. He told the members of the UN Security Council that Afghanistan "is challenged by the deterioration of the security environment which stems from daily harassment and intimidation [and] inter-ethnic and inter-factional strife."[44]

Eventually, however, the Bush administration says Afghanistan's security is up to the Afghans. Therefore, an Afghan National Army (ANA) and Afghan police will need to be developed and ready for duty when the temporary forces withdraw. To this end, President Hamid Karzai in November 2002 announced his intent to organize seventy thousand troops. So far, three thousand soldiers have been recruited and trained at the military training center in Kabul, but some of these new recruits have already quit because of low

International Security Assistance Force

The International Security Assistance Force (ISAF) was established by the United Nations Security Council to assist the new Afghan government with security and stability. The following countries contribute to the ISAF: Austria, Belgium, Bulgaria, Britain, the Czech Republic, Denmark, Finland, France, Germany, Greece, Italy, New Zealand, the Netherlands, Norway, Portugal, Romania, Spain, Sweden, and Turkey. Germany and the Netherlands military troops took over the command of the ISAF from Turkey, the only Muslim country to take part in the ISAF, in December 2002.

An ISAF soldier stands guard while villagers wait to receive winter clothing from a humanitarian organization.

The ISAF's task is to ensure freedom of movement in Kabul, to advise the Afghan government on security structures, to assist operation of Kabul International Airport, and to assist in the construction of an Afghan national force. During its operations ISAF has trained Afghan members of the Afghan National Guard and completed several hundred humanitarian aid projects.

pay. The task of rebuilding an entire new military and police force is a relatively long-term project, and it will take many years before the Afghan army is a reality.

Efforts are also under way for the implementation of the Disarmament, Demobilization, and Reintegration (DDR) program. The purpose of this program is to promote countrywide disarmament by helping former combatants find jobs and return to civilian life. This too will be a difficult program to implement, however. Regional warlords such as Dostum in the north and the governor of Herat, Ismail Khan, have thus far refused to disarm their private armies. So far the government believes that working with the warlords, despite their past atrocities, is necessary for the future stability of the country.

Creation of a Broad-Based Government

Rebuilding the national armed forces alone cannot bring peace and prosperity unless accompanied by political reform. In December 2001 the United Nations sponsored a conference in Bonn, Germany, on the future of Afghanistan. Representatives of various Afghan factions attended the conference. The accord called for the establishment of a thirty-member Afghan Interim Authority (AIA), with Karzai as its president, to govern the country for six months.

In accordance with another provision of the accord, a *Loya Jirga* (Grand Council) met in Kabul from June 10 to June 21, 2002. The *Loya Jirga* members selected an Afghan Transition Authority (ATA) to lead Afghanistan, pending the election of a fully representative government within two years. The members of the *Loya Jirga* approved Karzai as the head of the ATA.

Under the Bonn agreement, the constitution is to provide a framework for new elections to be held in 2003. A nine-member drafting commission has recently completed a proposed constitution. Another thirty-five member commission will lead a public debate process, where members of the public will have the opportunity to express their views on the constitution before the five-hundred delegates to the *Loya Jirga* ratify it in October 2003. National elections are scheduled for June 2004.

Critics express concern about the hurried pace of producing a new constitution. Unless the international community helps the Afghan government contain the power of the warlords, critics worry the central government may not be powerful enough to successfully implement the new constitution.

Paying the Bill

Another crucial ingredient for future peace and prosperity in Afghanistan is reconstruction of the economy. The long-term cost of rebuilding war-torn Afghanistan has been estimated at more than $50 billion over the next decade. Many countries, nongovernmental organizations, and international organizations will play crucial roles in the economic development of Afghanistan. They will provide multibillion dollars in loans and grants to the struggling nation.

At the International Conference on Reconstruction Assistance to Afghanistan held in Tokyo, January 21–22, 2002, the international

Afghan children rejoice during a ceremony to mark the reopening of their school in Kabul.

community pledged some $4.5 billion for the next five years, and as much as $1.8 billion for 2002. The World Bank has offered $100 million in grants to Afghanistan. The United Nations has reportedly spent $1.2 billion in 2002 on reconstruction and aid, which has resulted in 3 million students going back to school, 60 miles of road being built, and 2 million jobs created. In addition Bush signed the Afghanistan Freedom Support Act into law in December 2002, authorizing $3.3 billion in U.S. economic, political, humanitarian, and security assistance for Afghanistan over the next four years.

So far reconstruction has not taken place. The big projects, roads, irrigation, and rural development have remained on paper. Most observers attribute the lack of reconstruction in Afghanistan as the failure of donor countries to meet their pledges, the slow pace of financial aid, and the Afghan government's management failures and security problems.

The past two decades in the violent history of Afghanistan show that ethnicity and religion have been very influential forces that have prevented a national consciousness from developing. There is strong consternation that similar conditions may prevail in the post-Taliban leadership unless the government addresses this crucial issue. In order for Afghanistan to escape its past and create a civil society, a balance of power must be brokered among competing ethnic and religious groups so that no particular identifiable group possesses more power and authority than others.

At the dawn of the twenty-first century, Afghanistan is at another crossroad. It is faced with the task of rebuilding a civil society, security, political institutions, and economic infrastructure. Moreover, Afghans have to lay the foundation of a new political and economic system in order to help the country achieve long-term peace and prosperity. Achieving peace and prosperity demands transfer of power from warlords to the elected representatives of the people and creation of a strong central government with its own national army and police. Last but not least, Afghanistan desperately needs the continued and sustained support of the world community. Without its support Afghanistan is bound to repeat its past mistakes.

Notes

Chapter One: The Great Game: Colonial Struggle for Afghanistan

1. Vartan Gregorian, *The Emergence of Modern Afghanistan: Politics of Reform and Modernization, 1880–1946.* Palo Alto, CA: Stanford University Press, 1969, pp. 111–12.

2. Abdul Samad Ghous, *The Fall of Afghanistan: An Insider's Account.* New York: Pergamon-Brassey, 1988, p. 3.

3. Sayed S. Hussain, Abdul H. Alvi, and Absar H. Rizvi, *Afghanistan Under the Soviet Occupation.* Islamabad: World Affairs Publications, 1980, p. 68.

4. Hussain et al., *Afghanistan Under the Soviet Occupation,* p. 71.

5. Mohammad Daud Miraki, "Factors of Underdevelopment in Afghanistan, 1919–2000," Ph.D. diss., University of Illinois, 2000, p. 82.

6. Richard Newell, *The Politics of Afghanistan.* Ithaca, NY: Cornell University Press, 1972, p. 44.

Chapter Two: A New Game: The Cold War

7. Barnett R. Rubin, *The Fragmentation of Afghanistan: State Formation and Collapse in the International System.* New Haven, CT: Yale University Press, 1995, p. 20.

8. Miraki, "Factors of Underdevelopment in Afghanistan, 1919–2000," pp. 208–209.

9. Riffat Sardar, "Soviet Intervention in Afghanistan and Its Implications for Pakistan," Ph.D. diss., University of Massachusetts, 1985, p. 58.

10. Muhammad Azmi, "Soviet Politico-Military Penetration in Afghanistan, 1955 to 1979," *Armed Forces and Society,* vol. 12, no. 3, Spring 1986, p. 334.

11. Anthony Arnold, *The Soviet Invasion in Perspective.* Stanford, CA: Hoover Institution Press, 1985, p. 84.

12. Quoted in Henry S. Bradsher, *Afghanistan and the Soviet Union.* Durham, NC: Duke University Press, 1985, p. 15.

13. Mark Huband, *Warriors of the Prophet: The Struggle for Islam.* Boulder, CO: Westview, 1998, p. 2.

14. Quoted in Rosanne Klass, ed., *Afghanistan: The Great Game Revisited.* New York: Freedom House, 1987, p. 15.

Chapter Three: The Taliban: From Chaos to Clampdown

15. Ahmed Rashid, *Taliban: Militant Islam, Oil, and Fundamentalism in Central Asia.* New Haven, CT: Yale University Press, 2001, p. 22.

16. Peter Marsden, *The Taliban: War, Religion, and the New Order in Afghanistan.* New York: Zed, 1998, p. 61.

17. Leila Helms, "Living Under the Taliban," MSNBC, April 3, 1999. www.msnbc.com.

18. Barnett R. Rubin, "Women and Pipeline: Afghanistan's Proxy War," *International Affairs,* vol. 73, no. 2, 1997, p. 294.

19. *World Press Review,* "The Taliban's Terror," August 1996, pp. 34–35.

20. Amnesty International, "Women in Afghanistan," 1996. www.amnesty.org.

21. Ziaba Shorish-Shamly, "Living in Fear," Silicon Village. www.village.co.uk.

22. Saira Shah, "A Personal Journey," Channel 4. www.channel4.com.

Chapter Four: A Diverse Nation

23. Leon B. Poullada, *Reform and Rebellion in Afghanistan, 1919–1929.* Ithaca, NY: Cornell University Press, 1973, p. 16.

24. Grant Farr, "The Hazara of Central Afghanistan." Hazara.org. www.hazara.org.

25. Farr, "The Hazara of Central Afghanistan."

26. Poullada, *Reform and Rebellion in Afghanistan, 1919–1929,* p. 21.

27. Sultan A. Aziz, "Pashtun Political Tribal Structure: Barrier to Soviet Penetration," Master's thesis, Bowling Green State University, 1984, p. 14.

Chapter Five: Women in Afghanistan

28. Huma Ahmed Ghosh, "Feminist Perspective: September 11th and Afghan Women," *Lemar-Aftaab,* January/February 2001, p. 3.

29. Fahima Vorgetts, "A Vision of Justice, Equality, and Peace," *Women for Afghan Women: Shattering Myths and Claiming the Future,* edited by Sunita Mehta. New York: Palgrave Macmillan, 2002, p. 94.

30. Erika Knabe, "Afghan Women: Does Their Role Change?" *Afghanistan in the 1970s,* edited by Louis Dupree and Linette Albert. New York: Praeger, 1974, p. 153.

31. Jan Goodwin, *Price of Honor: Muslim Women Lift the Veil of Silence on the Islamic World.* New York: Penguin, 1994, p. 95.

32. Rubin, *The Fragmentation of Afghanistan,* p. 80.

33. Goodwin, *Price of Honor,* p. 92.

34. Goodwin, *Price of Honor,* p. 92.

35. Knabe, "Afghan Women," p. 154.

36. Senzil Nawid, "Aman-Allah and the Afghan 'Ulama: Reaction to Reforms, 1919–29," Ph.D. diss., University of Arizona, 1987, p. 211.

37. Quoted in Nancy Hatch Dupree, "Revolutionary Rhetoric and Afghan Women," *Afghanistan Council,* occasional paper, no. 23, 1981, p. 2.

38. Parwin Ali Majrooh, "Afghan Women Between Marxism and Islamic Fundamentalism," *Central Asian Survey,* vol. 8, no. 3, 1989, p. 94.

39. Dupree, "Revolutionary Rhetoric and Afghan Women," p. 2.

40. Nancy Hatch Dupree, "Afghanistan Women Under the Taliban," *Fundamentalism Reborn: Afghanistan and the Taliban,* edited by William Maley. New York: New York University Press, 1998, p. 145.

41. Saira Shah, "Behind the Veil," June 27, 2001. http://news.bbc.co.uk.

42. Yuka Tachibana, "Afghan Women Defy Taliban," MSNBC, October 5, 2001. www.msnbc.com.

43. Rashid, *Taliban,* p. 110.

Epilogue: Rebuilding for Peace

44. Judy Aita, "UN Envoy Warns Security Problems Threatening Afghan Peace Process," U.S. Diplomatic Mission to Pakistan, May 7, 2003. http://usembassy.state.gov.

Chronology

1747
The modern nation of Afghanistan founded; Ahmed Shah Durrani becomes the first king of Afghanistan.

1839
The First Anglo-Afghan War starts.

1878
The Second Anglo-Afghan War begins.

1893
The Durand Line fixes the southern and eastern borders between Afghanistan and British India (currently Pakistan).

1919
Afghanistan secures its independence; Treaty of Rawalpindi gives Afghanistan control of its domestic and foreign policies.

1923
Afghanistan adopts its first constitution.

1934
United States recognizes Afghanistan.

1953
Prince Muhammad Daud becomes prime minister.

1959
Women appear unveiled in public for the first time.

1964
The *Loya Jirga* unanimously adopts a new constitution.

1965
The first nationwide parliamentary elections are held under the new constitution.

1973
Prince Muhammad Daud overthrows the monarchy in a military coup.

1978

Prince Muhammad Daud is overthrown in a bloody Communist military coup.

1979

Hafizullah Amin assassinates President Noor Mohammed Taraki; the Soviet Union invades Afghanistan.

1980

Pro-Moscow Afghan Communist, Babrak Karmal, becomes president.

1986

Najibullah Ahmedzai replaces Babrak Karmal as president.

1989

Last contingent of the Soviet occupying forces leaves Afghanistan.

1992

The mujahideen take Kabul, and Burhanuddi Rabbani becomes president. Civil war ensues.

1996

The Taliban militias drive President Burhanuddi Rabbani out of Kabul, capture the capital, and execute Najibullah Ahmedzai.

2001

The Northern Alliance militia and the American special forces defeat the Taliban forces; the UN-sponsored conference in Bonn brings together hostile Afghan ethnic groups to discuss post-Taliban Afghanistan.

2002

The *Loya Jirga* is convened in Kabul and elects Hamed Karzai president.

For Further Reading

Books

Martin Ewans, *Afghanistan: A Short History of Its People and Politics.* New York: HarperCollins, 2002. This book covers the political history of Afghanistan. It shows how centuries of invasion, fierce tribal rivalries, and powerful dynasties led to the creation of Afghanistan.

Vartan Gregorian, *The Emergence of Modern Afghanistan: Politics of Reform and Modernization, 1880–1946.* Palo Alto, CA: Stanford University Press, 1969. This book deals with the socioeconomic and political transformation of Afghan society from the late nineteenth century to the mid-twentieth century.

M. Hassan Kakar, *The Soviet Invasion and the Afghan Response, 1979–1982.* Berkeley: University of California Press, 1995. The book is an account of what happened in Afghanistan following the Soviet occupation. It focuses on the freedom fighters, summarizing their ideas and tracing the conflicts between them and traditional leaders.

Rosanne Klass, ed., *Afghanistan: The Great Game Revisited.* New York: Freedom House, 1987. This book is a collection of essays by several authors. The contributors focus on historical perspective to explain the Soviet decision to go into Afghanistan.

Websites

Afghanistan—A Country Study (http://lcweb2.loc.gov). The site is produced by the Library of Congress and covers all aspects of Afghan life, including culture, society, groups, and religion.

Afghanistan Online (www.afghan-web.com). Afghanistan Online provides updated news and information on Afghanistan's culture, history, and politics.

Afghanland (www.afghanland.com). This website consists of several informative sections related to Afghan literature, Afghan artists, news in Dari, activities of the International Security Assistance Force, and series of photos of historical buildings and scenes from the civil war.

Institute for Afghan Studies (www.institute-for-afghan-studies. org). This is an independent organization founded and run by Afghan scholars around the world to disseminate information for Afghan studies.

U.S. Agency for International Development—Helping Afghanistan (www.usaid.gov). This U.S. government site provides background information on the crisis and detailed information on American efforts to help the people of Afghanistan.

U.S. Department of State (www.state.gov). This U.S. government site contains country-specific information and useful links.

Works Consulted

Books

Anthony Arnold, *The Soviet Invasion in Perspective.* Stanford, CA: Hoover Institution Press, 1985. This book traces Soviet-Afghan relations since 1919 with emphasis on recent events leading to the Communist coup and the Soviet invasion.

Henry S. Bradsher, *Afghanistan and the Soviet Union.* Durham, NC: Duke University Press, 1985. This book is considered to be the authoritative source on the history of the Soviet intervention and its impact on the rest of the world.

Louis Dupree, *Afghanistan.* Princeton, NJ: Princeton University Press, 1980. This book is the most comprehensive source of information on Afghanistan up to the Soviet occupation.

Nancy Hatch Dupree, "Afghanistan Women Under the Taliban," *Fundamentalism Reborn: Afghanistan and the Taliban.* Ed. William Maley. New York: New York University Press, 1998. A look at women under the Taliban.

Abdul Samad Ghous, *The Fall of Afghanistan: An Insider's Account.* New York: Pergamon-Brassey, 1988. The book provides the reader with historical and political background from the early 1800s to the fall of President Daud's government in Afghanistan.

Larry P. Goodson, *Afghanistan's Endless War: State Failure, Regional Politics, and Rise of the Taliban.* Seattle: University of Washington Press, 2001. This book offers a concise analysis of what has happened since the Soviets invaded Afghanistan. It includes detailed discussions of ethnic, religious, social, and geographical cleavages in Afghan history.

Jan Goodwin, *Price of Honor: Muslim Women Lift the Veil of Silence on the Islamic World.* New York: Penguin, 1994. The author chronicles her journey to ten Muslim countries of the Middle East and North Africa.

Vartan Gregorian, *The Emergence of Modern Afghanistan: Politics of Reform and Modernization, 1880–1946.* Palo Alto, CA: Stanford University Press, 1969. This book deals with the socio-economic and political transformation of Afghan society from the late nineteenth century to the mid-twentieth century.

Mark Huband, *Warriors of the Prophet: The Struggle for Islam.* Boulder, CO: Westview, 1998. The author explains how Western powers have contributed to the rise of Islamic movements by their support of the mujahideen in Afghanistan.

Sayed S. Hussain, Abdul H. Alvi, and Absar H. Rizvi, *Afghanistan Under the Soviet Occupation.* Islamabad: World Affairs Publications, 1980. The authors provide a detailed discussion of British strategies adopted in Afghanistan to prevent Russian influence.

Rosanne Klass, ed., *Afghanistan: The Great Game Revisited.* New York: Freedom House, 1987. This book contains a collection of essays by several authors. The contributors focus on historical perspective to explain the Soviet decision to invade Afghanistan.

Erika Knabe, "Afghan Women: Does Their Role Change?" *Afghanistan in the 1970s.* Eds. Louis Dupree and Linette Albert. New York: Praeger, 1974. This book looks at Afghanistan in the 1970s, including the changing roles of women and students, political development, economic expansion, and evolution of literature, art, and music.

Peter Marsden, *The Taliban: War, Religion, and the New Order in Afghanistan.* New York: Zed, 1998. The book offers an overview of the historical and religious background of the Taliban.

Richard Newell, *The Politics of Afghanistan.* Ithaca, NY: Cornell University Press, 1972. This book studies political and economic developments in Afghanistan from 1963 to 1972.

Leon B. Poullada, *Reform and Rebellion in Afghanistan, 1919–1929.* Ithaca, NY: Cornell University Press, 1973. This book deals with King Amanullah. Poullada considers him as the most talented, liberal, and dynamic modernizer of Asia.

Leon B. Poullada and Leila D.J. Poullada, *The Kingdom of Afghanistan and the United States, 1828–1973.* Lincoln: University of Nebraska at Omaha, 1995. This book is a combination of memoirs, personal recollections, and academic scholarship. It is a historical study of the relationship between the United States and Afghanistan.

Ahmed Rashid, *Taliban: Militant Islam, Oil, and Fundamentalism in Central Asia.* New Haven, CT: Yale University Press, 2001. The book is an extensive account of the Taliban movement and their origin, interpretation of Islam, women, and society.

Olivier Roy, *Islam and Resistance in Afghanistan.* Cambridge: Cambridge University Press, 1985. This book examines the history, ideology, and structures of the Afghan resistance against the Soviet occupation of Afghanistan.

Barnett R. Rubin, *The Fragmentation of Afghanistan: State Formation and Collapse in the International System.* New Haven, CT: Yale University Press, 1995. The book argues that Afghanistan had to rely on foreign aid because the Afghan economy failed to generate a large amount of revenue.

Fahima Vorgetts, "A Vision of Justice, Equality, and Peace," *Women for Afghan Women: Shattering Myths and Claiming the Future.* Ed. Sunita Mehta. New York: Palgrave Macmillan, 2002. This book consists of insightful articles on the situation of women in Afghanistan.

Periodicals

Muhammad Azmi, "Soviet Politico-Military Penetration in Afghanistan, 1955 to 1979," *Armed Forces and Society,* vol. 12, no. 3, Spring 1986.

Nancy Hatch Dupree, "Revolutionary Rhetoric and Afghan Women," *Afghanistan Council,* occasional paper, no. 23, 1981.

Huma Ahmed Ghosh, "Feminist Perspective: September 11th and Afghan Women," *Lemar-Aftaab,* January/February 2001.

Ali A. Jalali, "Afghanistan in 2002: The Struggle to Win Peace," *Asian Survey,* vol. 43, no. 1, January/February 2002.

Parwin Ali Majrooh, "Afghan Women Between Marxism and Islamic Fundamentalism," *Central Asian Survey,* vol. 8, no. 3, 1989.

Alam Payind, "Soviet-Afghan Relations: From Cooperation to Occupation," *International Journal of Middle East,* vol. 21, no. 1, February 1989.

Barnett R. Rubin, "Women and Pipeline: Afghanistan's Proxy War," *International Affairs,* vol. 73, no. 2, 1997.

World Press Review, "The Taliban's Terror," August 1996.

Dissertations and Theses

Sultan A. Aziz, "Pashtun Political Tribal Structure: Barrier to Soviet Penetration." Master's thesis, Bowling Green State University, 1984. This study addresses the Soviet attempt to penetrate and control the Pashtun tribes in Afghanistan.

Mohammad Daud Miraki, "Factors of Underdevelopment in Afghanistan, 1919–2000." Ph.D. diss., University of Illinois, 2000. This study evaluates several factors that may have influenced the underdevelopment of Afghanistan.

Senzil Nawid, "Aman-Allah and the Afghan 'Ulama: Reaction to Reforms, 1919–29." Ph.D. diss., University of Arizona,

1987. The study focuses on the reign of King Amanullah and his failure to achieve his modernization programs.

Riffat Sardar, "Soviet Intervention in Afghanistan and Its Implications for Pakistan." Ph.D. diss., University of Massachusetts, 1985. This study investigates whether the Soviet intervention in Afghanistan was a threat to the neighboring country of Pakistan and how it affected Pakistan's relations with other countries.

Internet Sources

Grant Farr, "The Hazara of Central Afghanistan," Hazara.org. www.hazara.org.

Leila Helms, "Living Under the Taliban," MSNBC, April 3, 1999. www.msnbc.com.

Saira Shah, "Behind the Veil," June 27, 2001. http://news.bbc.co.uk.

———, "A Personal Journey," Channel 4. www.channel4.com.

Ziaba Shorish-Shamly, "Living in Fear," Silicon Village. www.village.co.uk.

Yuka Tachibana, "Afghan Women Defy Taliban," MSNBC, October 5, 2001. www.msnbc.com.

Index

Britain
  buffer state policy of,
    19–20
  "forward policy" of, 12–13
  interest of, in region, 12
  "stationary policy" of, 16
  see also Anglo-Afghan
    Wars
British India, rivalry with
  Russia and, 10
Buddha statues, destruction
  of, 48, 49
Bush, George W., 92

capitalism vs. communism,
  23
Cavagnari, Louis, 18
Central Intelligence Agency
  (CIA)
  assistance to mujahideen by,
    36–37
  implication of Taliban in
    terrorist acts and, 54
chador, 76, 84
Chagatai, 60
Cold War, 23–26
Conolly, Arthur, 10
Constitution of 1964, 59
  equal rights guaranteed in,
    72
  women's rights under,
    79–81

Dari (language), 59
  origin of, 61
Daud Khan, Muhammad, 29,
  30
  liberation of Afghan women
    under, 78–79
Declaration of Afghan

Women's Rights, 87
Democratic Organization of
  Afghan Women (DOAW),
  81
Disarmament,
  Demobilization, and
  Reintegration (DDR)
  program, 90
divorce, 75
Dost Muhammad Khan, 13
Dostum, Abdul Rashid, 70,
  90
Dupree, Louis, 13
Dupree, Nancy Hatch, 81
Durand, Henry Mortimer, 20,
  21
Durand Agreement (1893),
  20–21
Durand Line, 20, 21

East India Company, 12
education
  for girls
    under Amanullah Khan, 77
    under Taliban, 50, 83
  Soviet-U.S. aid for, 25–26

Farr, Grant, 61, 65

Gandamak, Treaty of (1879),
  17
Geneva Accords (1988), 38
Ghosh, Huma Ahmed, 72
Goodwin, Jan, 73, 74, 75
Gorbachev, Mikhail, 38
Great Game, 10, 11–13
  ending of, 22
Gregorian, Vartan, 13

Hazaras, 59–61

Picture Credits

About the Author

Hamed Madani is a professor of political science at Tarrant County College in Arlington, Texas. He has been writing and lecturing on Afghanistan politics and teaching American politics and American foreign policy for more than twenty years. He is a native of Afghanistan.